SCARRED TISSUE

"Underneath It All"

By: LaShanta D. Whitted

Book Cover by [HueCreativewing/ Fiverr]

Illustrations by [LaShanta. D. Whitted]

[1st] edition [2023]

I Dedicated this book to:

Carolyn Ann McMillan (Mom)

Thank you for instilling in me the gift of expression, the gift of strength, and courage to express even when I was voiceless. You always emphasized the importance of the matters of the heart while ensuring that I lead with GOD first. You always referenced the phrase: "You always know its GOD when……." and you would end the sentence with a situational occurrence that reminded me of where I need to align myself at all times. You always said HE will hear my cry with or without sound. Thank You Mom for always directing me even when I wanted to steer left.

To my Darling Children: Tyrone, Kyanna, Tracy, Tiffany, Lin,

Thank you for allowing me to have purpose. It is because of your unconditional love that I am here and still standing. Fighting the good fight and never backing down. No matter what the battle, we still continued to march forward with our heads held high, and never looking backwards. Thank you for making me hold to my words by never breaking promises.

Ernestine "Tina" Brown,

Well lady, where do I begin! You have made sure that I don't forget, "Who I am," "Where I currently am," and 'Where I need to be going". Thank you for the growth. Thank you for the open-door policy of honesty even when it hurt the most. Most importantly, THANK YOU, for reminding me that my self-worth and value matters most even when others don't appreciate me for ME! Thank you for helping me perfect my craft and giving me the guidance to complete it!

Alize King

Thank you for being one of my biggest fans. Thank you for proofing and ensuring that I am politically correct with words being expelled. I truly am grateful for your heartwarming love and support. Thank you for making me great in this world!

Bobbi / Jennifer Meekins

Where do I begin! You both ensured that I didn't forget the "mentionables." Thank you for making me feel like this walk with GOD was ordained to be. Jennifer, you envisioned this going beyond, thank you for opening my eyes to what can be and speaking it into existence. I salute you both from the bottom of my heart.

TABLE OF CONTENTS

PREFACE

Abuse

Relationship Abuse: *is a pattern of abusive and coercive behaviors used to maintain power and control over a former or current intimate partner*

Un: The Awakening

Yelling, Screaming, Shouting, Arguing

Swelling, Bruises, Punches, Holes, Broken Bones

Black Eyes, Busted Lips, Loss Teeth,

Stitches, Bandages, Band-aides, Wraps, Gauze

Tears, Fears, Intimidation, Anger, Hurt, Rage

Peace, Forgiveness, Withdrawal, Heartache, Pain

Survival!

Do any of this sound familiar? Do any of this remind you of your past or even your present-future situation? Are you the abuser or the one being abused? Self-identify your role in the madness. Picture yourself in the moment of abuse. Were you scared? Frightened? Forgiving? With so many emotions going through your mind at one time, one can only imagine if you would be able to answer any or all these questions at once, right? It is obvious that we fear the attacker, but should we ever become free from being attacked. At what point will we become the attacker ourselves? It's called self-defense. Fighting for your life to survive from being physically and mentally abused. We live uncaged and exhibit aggressive behavior through natural instincts that hunt our prey without cognitively thinking that we are enraged because we are tired of being abused. The adrenaline of the fight in us during the peak of fear, is what creates a stigmatism of being an abuser. Your word against theirs!

Repeating generational cycles tends to be one of the biggest excuses we use to continue the channel of abuse on one another. It has become second nature to find rational within that spectrum. The repeating of words heard and then used is the beginning of a systemic cycle of weakness. The mind plays a lot of tricks on us, don't it? This belief is most factual because society has led us to think that as a child what is witnessed is what is imitated, but at what point is the image corrected? Or will it ever be? We tend to forgive the abuser when they say, "I'm doing what I saw my uncle, father, or grandfather do." or "This is all I know." Were you really taught this behavior? Did someone sit you down and say this is how you do it? Were those words ever spoken in dialogue? Oftentimes, behaviors are imitated by what is seen and never corrected. We are misled to assume that things should be this way and this is why they are. Leaving scars upon scars to create scabs on wounds that have never healed is the constant reminder in the victim's daily walk for the rest of their life. They too played into the systemic cycle of weakness. Seeing others perform acts of violence on the innocent or not so innocent makes it easier to violate. When you witnessed the abuser abusing another, did you speak up and say "STOP!" or "This is wrong!" If you didn't, then you were just as guilty for the harm being done as the abuser throwing the punches.

There are many different dynamics that are contributors to abuse besides generational cycles. Issues within the home or everyday walk-in life such as stress, finances, kids, divorce, job loss, drug/alcohol abuse or even mental health issues undiagnosed are just a few of the contributing factors as to what triggers an abuser to harm and hurt another. So, what's your reasoning for channeling your fist towards someone else's face, head, or body?

Deux: Climbing the Peak

What leads up to the rage? Do you know what sends you to the top of the volcano and erupt? What triggers your emotions to explode? Inside the belly of the volcano lies heat, fumes, and fire. Heat turns into fire. Fire turns into rage. That rage explodes. The boiling point of that rages seems uncontrolled, however, we can sometimes diffuse the fire with a water hose; a cooling agent, if you will. Can your fire be diffused and at what point can someone use water to diffuse it before it explodes?

In arguments, diffusion tactics are always a consideration. The fear of wanting to calm a person down before the attack is the natural instinct within us. We want peace. We want calm. We want to be rational with each other. We fear the unknown. The pleading and begging for understanding. The use of de-escalation tactics at times don't matter to the abuser. They feed off of the desires of not wanting to be harmed. The desire to want to live. They are driven by having the power to decide! The timeliness of our will power to cease and dismiss is what determines the cause and effect of their actions. We often-times refuse to allow diffusion before explosion. Often times, we add to the explosion by counter-acting our own emotions and feelings of whose wrong and whose right. But is it worth it in the end? Are we willing to face the repercussions from what we know can result in brutal punishment or even death? There are times when the eruption don't stem from your current situation but has been fueling from a different fire. The rage from the carryover! Are you the victim of a different circumstance? A compilation of things unknown but you take on the blame. Were you the one who caused the volcano to erupt? Or were you just the fire they wanted to burn in hell?

I experienced a lot of fights in my young adult life from relationships, fights in front of friends, family members, and children. Fights because I tried to save face. Fights unnecessarily, because the abuser told me that I was too weak and timid of a woman with the goal intended to make me stronger and fearless.

I was 18 years old, soft-spoken, a mother of 2 children, who didn't speak much and who always kept to herself. I knew my lane to walk in. I was a child. I wasn't into the everyday drama that most people subjected themselves to. I loved being alone and my home was my safe haven. My safe space from the ways of the world where no one could hurt or harm me. I wasn't very outgoing and neither was I outspoken. I was a far cry from the noticeable type. I couldn't stand looking at myself in the mirror. I hated taking pictures and hated the camera. I got teased a lot in school and at home as a young child, which caused me to have low self-esteem growing up. Building a wall around myself was comforting the more I went through relationships. The infidelity, the drugs, the drinking was a part of the package so I endured things with normalcy and grace. The relationship itself was all that mattered to me. Receiving the love and the feeling of it added completeness that I longed for. BUT it wasn't love enough to stop the pain!

I was seven years his senior and "green as grass" as they called me. My perception was, the older the man, the more mature the man would be. The older the man would bring more security and less bullshit. I was so wrong! It brought more control. Control of ME! I was naive to the ways of the world and was raised from a different cloth. A southern cloth. That was his advantage! I found myself in a triangle of deciding to leave or stay and the options were few. If I left, then my children would suffer and not be taken care of like I needed them too financially. If I stayed, then I would continue dealing with all the sins of the relationship. I was tired and felt that enough was enough. I finally had gotten up enough strength to speak my voice. Finally courage had outweighed fear. All I wanted to do was go and get my children from the sitter and make my own way. I had gotten off work around 11:30pm and I headed to pick up my children. There were so many arguments during the day between us but all I knew was that I was tired! I was blamed for having someone in my ear putting me up to wanting to walk away. The threats of violence towards me had I went through with my plans, was a constant reminder of what I endured all these years. I just wanted it to stop! I wanted out! He would often tell me that I couldn't do nothing for them. I wasn't strong enough of a woman to raise children. The constant threats of making my life miserable if they were found to be suffering in any way, was my confirmation to walk way. The belittling tactics of losing control, I found, was a sign of his weakness, not mines. I knew that I could manage but the opposing saw me as a weak vessel, not unfit, but weak as a person. I had gotten tired and wanted to be alone. I was much stronger than he had given credit for. I was stronger than he ever knew. I had gotten a call from his sitter saying that he had picked up the children a few hours earlier than normal. That infuriated me! I knew what I had coming to me when I got off work, but I was so up for the challenge, NO MATTER WHAT! The freedom for me and my babies was well worth the fight. I called him to see why he picked up my babies from the sitter and where had he taken them. I didn't have much money for a cab to go to his sister's house and then home, so I asked my coworker to lend me some money until payday. My heart was racing so fast at the thought of getting into another fight with him that I started shaking uncontrollably. The more I spoke, the more I trembled as I was trying to explain to my coworker all that I have been going through these past few years. About how he would come up to my job and sit in the back corners and wait for me to get off without ever letting me know he was there. Then he would walk far behind me to ensure that I went in the house from work late at night. Like a stalker. The more I explained, the more she started putting two and two together regarding my actions and behavior. I had a lot of dark days with this man but this was my fight and my fight alone. Tonight, it had to end. Tonight I was through, no matter what became of this situation!

I quickly called a cab and headed over to his sister's house. He was standing outside talking to his parents as they sat in their car. My babies laid in the back seat asleep. As soon as I had gotten out of the cab, he began yelling at me, "Get back in the cab and go home!" He said I wasn't getting my babies back. I knew that this was his way of making me stay with him and continue the daily drama. The control an abuser has is what we will never relinquish. It gives him power. Most importantly, POWER over you! I walked over to the car and began talking to his parents about how I felt. Pleading with them to understand. As I was speaking, he pushed me to the ground. I quickly jumped to my feet. Crying and yelling for him to get my babies out of the car. I was frantic but before I could get near the car, a backhand slap came across my face. He had no issue with hitting me in front of his parents, and they didn't stop him at all. It was as if, they weren't even there. As they sat in silence, watching, no one would show me defense and make him stop. This repeated cycle of abuse seemed to be a trended cycle within the family of the men versus their women. Men were the dominant factor by all means and this was their way of controlling their households. I was a thin framed woman and his size and statue made two of me. I didn't stand a chance if I should have ever fought him back. At times, I was very scared of him, but not this time. He kept saying, "That's why I beat your ass because you are too fucking timid for me. Look at you, you won't even fight me back!" But I couldn't fight back. All I could do was think of the last times he hit me. The punches, the pain, the bruises. I didn't know where to start and I wasn't the kind of woman who allowed my anger to hit that boiling point until now. When he said those words, I became angrier and angrier. As I stood there, the rage fueled quickly inside of me, line an erupted volcano. I swung as hard as I could with a closed fist. I hit him in the jaw! OMG, I hit his big ass! For the first time, I fought him back and I couldn't stop swinging. We were fighting like we didn't even know each other. I got angry and I grew tired. I wasn't going to go home with another bruise on my face, and arms. I wasn't going to wake up in pain again over some foolishness. I was too damn tired of it. Then I heard a stern voice say, "You two better stop it and get in this car!" Well, his parent finally speaks after they saw that I'm fighting their precious child back, but it was ok when he was whooping my ass all these years. Like, Really! The bullshit doesn't cease to amaze me. Once he heard his parent speak, he stopped and looked at me. I looked at him and said, "Now give me my babies!" His parent asked us to get in the car and because it was late, he said he was taking me home. I couldn't believe what came over me. For an instance, I liked who I had just become and at that point I knew I no longer feared what the devil tried to bring my way. I had the fight in me that I didn't know existed. I now know I am strong enough to walk away without fear, especially fear of abuse. GOD stepped in and gave me the courage I needed to win and end years of physical hurt and pain. HE gave me the strength to be a protector and provider of my children. Mankind did not have a hold of my heart any longer because I was now stronger than I had ever been, and it felt damn good to be on the winning side of things. For the sake of loving, is the reason we accept? As we say, especially for the kids, until GOD steps in and have the final word!

1 John 4:9 Parents are introduced to a kind of love they could never have imagined once their baby arrives. This amazing love is made possible by the love that the Lord has so generously lavished on us.

Trois: When the Bow Breaks

We never know the day nor the hour until our Faith has been tested. But what is a test? Truly what does it mean to be "tested"? How do we overcome such obstacles? Several years went by, we grew to get to know each other from a different perspective. Respecting each other was key. We became wiser and put what was most important first, our family!

It was a warm Sunday afternoon. My babe and I had decided to go out for dinner with the kids. It was a long time coming and the night couldn't have been more perfect. As the night grew darker, we decided to go home and get the kids ready for bed. We hadn't spent much time together, so every minute alone mattered. We took advantage of every opportunity to spend time together for the sake of the relationship. He was a great dad and wonderful soon-to-be husband. I never thought I could find someone who has grown to be so as loving as he was to me. GOD gave me a good man and provider. I never had to work but I chose to do so. I wanted to have my own sense of independence just in case I had to do it all over again on my own. He made sure I finished High School and went on to college. He picked up a job working at night and took care of the kids during the day. We managed to keep the household expenses low. Preparing for the future was the focus. However, tomorrow was the day for new beginnings. It was his first day on dayshift at his new job and my first day at Hair School as a cosmetologist. He expressed the importance of having backup trade just in case one of us ever became out of work. He always spoke about how having a secondary trade would always ensure that you would make ends-meet during the rough times. He always said "we wouldn't be around forever, so we must plan ahead." It was another tell-tell sign that GOD was trying to prepare me for. But was I paying attention? I refused to entertain the thought that one day, we wouldn't be here. Can you imagine the thought of never being here on earth? I never allowed him to finish the sentence when he spoke like that. Naturally, one day we all will have the timer on our clocks shut off, but by GODs grace, HE will prolong that clock for as long as possible. We had 2 children ages 4 and 5 years of age. Yes, our hands were full but we enjoyed every bit of it. They were right behind each other in age so much so that they are the same age for 2 ½ weeks, yet they are not twins. They truly got a kick out of that and I always shook my head at the foolery of it all. But that was love before, during, and after everything else.

"Baby", I spoke softly: "How about you get the kids ready for bed while I get comfortable for our bed." I said to him. "OH YEAH" he replied with a grin on his face. He stood 6"4 in height and 276 lbs. in weight. Yes, this was my kind of man! By this time, it was 11p.m. We had finally got the kids to sleep, and we now have time alone. I didn't care about the time because it was a start to our new beginning.

As we both lay in each other's arms we were awaken by the alarm clock, our oldest daughter, she was 5 years old at the time. There she stood at the foot of the bed. "Mommy and Daddy, wake up" she exclaimed. I looked up at her and laid back down and said "Okay, sweety, go back in your room. We are getting up now, close my door, ok?" "Okayyyyy" she said softly as if we were bothering her. "Ma, that clock says 6 and a 4 and a 7. It got an "A" and an "M" at the end." So, as I heard her speak the words, I jumped up and nudged him to wake up. "Baby, get up. We are late. Come on baby, get up!" I yelled repeatedly. It was as if we had just fallen asleep, well we did around 3:00a.m. You would have thought he was dreaming because all he could think about was sex. By the time we did get out of bed, it was 7:12a.m. "Shaun" he yelled. "Get the kids ready while I get myself together and take a shower." "OK" I replied. "Baby I can't believe how late it is." I stated to him. He then replied hastily "Damn, fuck! See, Shaun this is exactly what I be talking about right here." He yelled.

So, as they prepared to exit the house, it was almost 8:00a.m. It was now time for me to get ready for school. I had to be there by 9:00a.m and Blanca usually gets here to pick me up by 8:30a.m. This morning I didn't have time for my daily news on Channel 5 or my 7-11 coffee run as usual. Ring, Ring, Ring. The house phone rang loudly. "Hello" I answered. "Hey Shaun, your bout ready?" says Blanca. "Yeah, give me 20 minutes and by the time you get here I will be coming downstairs." I replied. "OK, I will be there by 8:30." Blanca stated. 'OK" I said. As I hung up the phone, I cut on the TV and jumped in the shower. When I got dressed Blanca was already downstairs waiting for me. I ran out the door and forgot to cut off the lights, TV, and I even left the iron plugged up. "Blanca, give me a sec, I forgot to cut stuff off and he is already complaining about the high bills he got to pay." I stated to Blanca. "OK girl hurry up; you know we are running late as it is." Blanca replied. I ran quickly upstairs cutting everything off and unplugging all cords in sockets. As I got back in the car, Blanca just looked at me and spoke. "It's that serious huh." I replied "yes, but I feel so off balance because my morning ritual is messed up." I stated to her. She continues to speak with sternness in her voice, "It isn't nothing on TV but bad news, breaking news, shootings and killings, and most importantly, you need to STOP drinking that dang coffee" "Hell it makes you talk too much" she jokingly stated. After a good laugh, I then said "Well you're right, they were reporting bad stuff when I turned it off but at least I will know what's going on"

Upon arriving to school, I texted him, like I do every morning to let him know I arrived safely to any destination. I then contacted the school to check on the kids. They too had arrived safely. Their teacher Ms. Blessing wanted to know why this morning they were late for school. All I could do was laugh. It was now 11:30a.m and almost time for lunch break. Mrs. Aukenbaugh, our instructor, called me to the office right before our class dismissed for lunch. As I approached the office, I saw his sister sitting at the desk solemnly. "Hey girl" I said to her. "Why on earth are you here? It isn't Friday." I jokingly whispered in her ear. Friday's were our hair days where we work for tips doing clients hair for cheap price. She slowly stood to her feet with such a somber look in her red eyes. As she tried to speak, her voice cracked. She said "Shaun, I need to talk to you." The way she spoke brought cold chills all through my body. I immediately said "Why" as if I already knew she was going to tell me some bad news. So, as I looked out the window, I could see everybody in their cars lined up in front of my school as if they was going to a funeral or had just come from one. I then began to scream loudly: "WHAT HAPPENED, WHAT HAPPENED TO MY BABY!" It was then she said those words, those words that I never thought in a million years I would never hear. "He's dead Shaun, he's dead!" As she uttered those words it was as if I was hearing echoes in my mind. I quickly covered up my ears and blanked out. Those words that forever changed my life! I couldn't register those words with reality. Nothing could have prepared me for this. Nothing! I blanked out and I don't remember going into the break room. As I came out of it, I was lying on the floor in a fetal position while his sisters cradled me in her arms crying like a baby. I looked up and saw holes in the walls and lockers with dents in them. They say I blanked out and they couldn't control me, so they let me release my anger. He had been in a tragic car accident heading to work. He had just dropped the kids off at daycare and of course was running late. He collided head on with a tractor trailer from his job, and his car burst into flames. By-standers managed to free him, but it was too little too late. The breaking news that morning on Channel 5 was my love in a burning car. The news report showed rescuers trying to get him out while the car was on fire. Although he did survive, he would have been a vegetable. His parents took him off life support and didn't allow no one to see him.

Nothing, but nothing could have prepared me for this incident. I begged GOD to take this one back. I felt I wasn't ready to be alone and a single parent, but he prepared me and GOD used him as a vessel to do so. How was I going to do this? Who would help me? The pain was unimaginable. I oftentimes wondered about other situations and young mothers going through this heartache, but I never imagine that one day it would be me. He always said he wasn't going to be here forever and what he was showing me would only make me stronger. We often discussed the "what if's." A week prior to his death, he made me promise that should anything happen to him that I would ensure that the children grew to know his parents. It was as if GOD was telling me to be prepared for the inevitable. I honored his dying wishes until the passing of both his parents. They were an intricate part of our life and the kids' upbringing. I will forever be indebted to the both of them. Even though he is no longer with me in the physical realm, he is always with me spiritually every step I take!

Love Always
Mom and Pop

GOD prepares us for unforeseen circumstances. HE always sends us signs to get our attention even down to the smallest detail. The issue lies when we don't pay attention to those small details: The last words spoken, gestures, or even silences. I was prepared in more ways than one and it didn't start with this love story. I was prepared before the love ever existed. I just didn't realize the strength I had within me to continue the fight until I experienced my first loss, my first heartbreak. When your back is up against the wall, you either give up or push forward. There were so many positives in my life whereby I never felt like I lost anything. I learned so much from experiencing love and learning about love with this relationship. I was well prepared! My children were too young to know about death. It was my duty as the sole parent to ensure that they were taught the meaning of life and death in due time. That even with death, there is love. It is just felt in a different space and a different way.

By asking God for help regarding its reality, Moses makes a vital statement about preparing for death: "So teach us to number our days, that we may gain a heart of wisdom" Ecclesiastes 7:1-4

Quatre: The Cry of the Wolf

The physical abuse is just what it says. Physical means, "The act of force or forcing. Perception: to the body opposed to the mind by moving a person or one's own body with force."

Physical abuse can be objects hitting, punching, throwing, or grabbing someone in a harmful or hurtful way. Why do you feel the need to be abusive? Is it a form of communication or having control over another person that completes who you are as a lesser person? Perhaps, it is satisfaction for intimidation to the other or a form of weakness within you, the abuser.

Abuse is more than what it means: Having disregard for another person or thing. To hurt or harm; mentally or physically. We can abuse other people just as we can abuse the relationships with those people. Taking things for granted for lack of better understanding. To say someone abused you means they did harm to you without your permission. They are forcing you to act with self-defense no matter what harm is done to you, including death. Did you react or allow the abuse to take place? Are you the attacker or the victim? Did you provoke the attacker or were you provoked? Did you try to diffuse the situation before becoming abused or were you the abuser this time? Did the use of a fist or object to another person leave a mark intended or unintended? Bruised or blemished. What marks were left in the aftermath of the abuse after the swelling subsided? What color were the bruises? Blue, Black, or Red. Were you ashamed to look at them in the mirror or did you look in fright? Did you mean it when you said, "Enough is enough!" Questions upon questions racing through your mind. All to have no answers because of fear. Walking away seemed like enough, but did you forgive the abuser for the physical damage sustained mentally and physically and did you go back.

Being abused leaves the fear of retaliation to the other. There is a fear that brings silence in our daily walk of not wanting others to know what happened. Were you ashamed of what others may think or say about you? Most victims are ashamed and scared to speak out against their attacker. A cry out for help would have resolved a lot of anguish and saved a lot of heartaches and pain, but did you cry out or remain silent with a closed mouth? I had only one best friend in the world. My best friend had been with me through thick and thin. They even helped me do several things like: cover up the bruises, hid me from the world of humiliation, and healed my aches and pains with the exception of my heart. My best friend always spoke in silence and was my rock to lean on whenever I needed them the most. I never had to worry because my best friend gave me all I needed and more. My best friends name was CVS Pharmacy. The makeup isle turned my black and blues to browns. Helped turn my scars to scabs. They was always there for me, allowing me to cover up what my heart couldn't. That isle shielded me from embarrassment and kept me telling lies instead of living the truth. What or who was your best friend? The best part about it was that my best friend didn't charge me a lot of money to keep my secret near and dear to their heart. Inexpensive to say the least. How big was the price you had to pay for someone to keep your secret? Most importantly, was it worth it? Hoping that the abuse will subside, and the absence of memory would make things better. All you wanted to do was forget it ever happened. Remember, GOD gave us memory so we wouldn't forget for a reason. Why, of all people, did it happen to you? The words of outsiders seem to carry more weight than common sense. The name calling, insults of how others will think of you, knowing they are on the outside looking in, would make you walk away in silence and shame. Negative comments such as "You're stupid for putting up with it!" or "If it was me…" Prepare to know these comments are coming. Somebody is going to speak them or think them. It's expected that society was built that way. That shit never fails. But don't allow it to deter the victim from seeking help and assistance for fear of being shamed and insulted. Not wanting to feel any worse for dealing with the ordeal is the reason for the lack of communication to others. However, the abuser will play the "blame game" and make comments to the victim like: "It's your fault!" or "Look what you made me do!" The blame game will only add insult to injury on the part of the victim who will begin to feel like what is happening to them is truly their fault. They will rest with that mental theory until the act of forgiveness sets in. Ask yourself: How long will you continue to play the victim and accept that the matters of abuse are truly your fault? Vulnerability and the sense of not wanting to be alone are the biggest reasons we continue to accept! How many more beatings can you sustain before that one incident takes your life or those closest to you!

Cinq: The Raging Bull

It was a beautiful warm summer evening and I waited until the time was right to want a car. I had become depended on others along with public transportation for far too long. I just became a new homeowner and after reassessing my household expenses over 3 months, a new car would be fitting to complete the package. I was 22-years old, head strong woman and I was flying high. I had a good paying job with a stable mind. I knew my direction. I felt I had accomplished my goals at the tail end of an 8 year relationship that resulted in 2 marriage proposals with no wedding. It was clearly time for a change and a new look on my life. I wanted success and the cards dealt to me was that I had to do it alone but I was ok with that. Being a single mother with 4 children required strength, and patience. Strength to continue pushing day to day while having patience to endure it all without breaking and giving up. I remember times after my children were born and I couldn't afford more than one stroller. I would have to pack them all in one stroller, sitting one behind the other going to and from daily. That was my form of transportation.

I got up early that morning and dropped the kids off at their grandparents while I set out that day to go car shopping. I only wanted something small, low in monthly payments and maintenance. Just something for us to get around, nothing fancy or expensive. It was important that I stayed within what I could afford and ensured that I don't live beyond my means. That day I went to several dealerships comparing new cars versus used cars. I asked my dad for a few pointers about what I should look for. He insisted I carry a DO's and DON'T list so that I don't get trapped in the money game with dealerships. Car shopping gave me a sense of maturity. I wasn't relying on no one only myself. I was prepared and focus driven while walking with a sense of pride about my accomplishments this year. The blessings that were coming my way was mind boggling. I was so focused and focused indeed. I kept thinking about how many other twenty-two year olds bought a home in my circle or even generation. I felt such pride in knowing that my hard work truly did pay off. The smiles on my kid's faces was priceless when we moved in our new home. Smiling was something I wanted to ensure they have on a consistent basis. Freedom!

I didn't know what tomorrow would bring but I was enjoying every bit of it. There were many dark days and nights, but we made it through and finally it was about us. Or so I thought!

The next day, I got up and got the kids ready for school. I had taken the day off after receiving a call from a dealership who captured my online application. I was excited! Could today be the day I get my own car? I had a long way to go to get to the dealership. It took me an hour on public transportation to get there, but I made it for my 10:00a.m appt. I had made after school arrangements for the kids with my neighbor. I didn't know how long it would take but Evelyn was always there for us. She gave me all the support in the world and I couldn't have been more grateful for her. After meeting with the dealership, I informed them that I had no money down. The salesperson came back and asked me if I could put down $200 which would cover the tax and tags. I had $300 on me and I ecstatically said "Sure! I can do that!" OMG! Life just got a little bit easier for us. What a blessing! I couldn't believe it. I provided a roof over our heads, and I got a car. I called my neighbor to have her walk the kids over to the house as I was on my way back home with the car. I informed her that with traffic, I should be there in about forty-five minutes. Evelyn made sure the kids was safely in the house and locked all the doors until I got home. The traffic was a little heavy and that delayed me by about thirty more minutes getting home. As I sat in traffic, a sense of calm came over me. There were a lot of toxic days and nights alone, but I continued to pray that one day GOD would rescue me from the madness. He finally did when I began to listen. I worked 6 years as a Clerk with the Post Office and made a decent salary. Prior to purchasing my home, I ask my partner if that was something we could do to progress our union. He said "No, he wasn't ready to make such a big step." But I was. I was physically and mentally prepared for that. Prior to becoming interested in buying a home, I rented a three bedroom apartment paying $1600 a month plus utilities, so it all made sense to buy a home which lowered my monthly expenses to be able to buy a car. I had a candid conversation with my partner before pursuing my happiness and I realized we weren't on the same page with our future plans. I had to do what was best for me and my children. For an entire year, I went to look at houses with my realtor. On the morning of my 22nd birthday, I got up and told him I was going to the store, but instead my realtor was outside waiting to take me to closing. He thought the house we moved into was a rental and didn't even question any differently. I didn't address it any other way. Things were the way they were! I was yearning for more of what the good Lord was blessing me with. I centered my life around my church faith through reading and fasting. I was blessed with more than I could have ever asked for. GOD was my leader and there was no other way that I wanted to live my life and no other way I wanted my kids to lead theirs. Stepping out on faith was not a fear of mines but ensuring that I was no longer in bondage of abuse be it physical or mental. That hunger came with continuous obedience for what the good Lord could offer me. HE was my protector of my life: of whom shall I fear. (Psalm 27:1)

They say trouble will sometimes follow you and I was tired of living in the dark days of looking over my shoulder. Trying to feel safe. Many times, I accepted the blame for things that went wrong but as we know the abuser is one great manipulator. We know they have their own intentions and play mind games of manipulation when it came to continuing to feed their soul. But the "devil is a liar."

I arrived at home around 8p.m. from the dealership. I pulled up to my house and witnessed a shadow standing in the doorway. It was him. How did he get in my house? Why was he here? I sat in the car for a moment anticipating past outcomes and what might become of this. I wasn't up for any excuses, and I surely wasn't going to turn back now.

My life was going great. The kids and I was finally at a place of happiness and now we have the capabilities of going places and doing things together. He and I had separated almost a month ago and I didn't want to be in a relationship again especially not with him or anyone for that matter. Things had gone bad for a long time and all I wanted was my distance to clear my head and find me all over again. All the fights, bruises and scars, I truly remember everything like it was just yesterday, well at least that's how it felt. Have you ever been in a fight with someone when time as long past since it happened, but you still feel the tension, anger, punches as if it had just happened? Well, that's how I felt at the very moment I saw him in my doorway. Every time I looked in the mirror, I felt the punches. I felt the aches and pains. I saw the bruises healed and unhealed. I wanted no more. I gathered my things out of my car and proceeded to walk up the steps to my front door. There he stood, guarding the entrance into my home. I peeked inside the house and saw the kids sitting on the steps. They didn't appear to be happy. There was a somber look on all their faces. All I could do was wonder who let him in or for a lack of better words, why did he coarse the children to open the door. The known abuser most times know his victims. They know what to say and do to get what they want. They are

GREAT manipulators of the mind. They were children and knew nothing more than he was someone special to them. So naturally, they would open the door. They was never told differently no matter what our past held. We hadn't seen him in almost two months. What possibly could he want now? No phone calls or texts. Nothing. As I proceeded to walk in the house, I asked him angrily, "What are you doing in my house?" Why are you here?" He didn't respond or say a word. He stood there walking behind me as I put my things down. I walked over towards the children and asked them if they had their clothes together because I wanted to take them out for a little while. I hurried them upstairs to gather their things. I told them I would be up their shortly. As they hurried upstairs, I walked past him towards the living room. The smell of liquor and marijuana wreaked his clothes and the air space of my home. I stood before him and looked in his eyes, they were blood shot red in color. His eyes filled with rage. He appeared agitated and angry but from what I didn't know and didn't want to stick around to find out. I clearly knew that was danger was lurking in the air. I hadn't seen him in almost a month since our split and I didn't want any parts of what the past entailed. All I wanted was for him to leave my home and leave peacefully, just as peacefully as when we separated two months ago. It was amicable and I wanted today to be the same way. Why would it not be? There were no arguments, fights, or threats of violence. Only complete silence and I loved it. I finally had peace to think and plan my life going forward. The past is not where I wanted to continue to live. I channeled my energy to focus on positive things. GODLY things. As I walked to my room to put my papers away, he spoke with such discernment, "Where have you been?" I replied, "Why? Why are you here?" He refused to answer the question and instead he replied, "Where have you been, I'm just asking you a simple question?" I became hesitant to answer him after looking at the rage in his eyes. The volcano was erupting and it was nothing I could to do to try and diffuse the fire. He came for trouble, and I didn't want to tell him I bought a new car. I feared what he would do to it. I didn't want him to try and take it. So, I kept quiet and let him continue to rant. I knew there was nothing I could say or do to stop the volcano from erupting. At this point my hands were tired with what steps to take next or words to say to redirect his mindset. "I checked your answering machine, and some dude wants you to call him?" Who the hell is the dude calling your phone?" I looked at him and I spoke with no knowledge of what he was talking about. "What dude are you talking about?" I frantically responded. Confused as to who he was talking about. My heart began racing but not because I had something to hide but because of this aggressive behavior. I was scared beyond. Scared at this point while trying to figure out his next move. I just wanted to grab my babies and run out of the house, but I froze. I couldn't move and I clearly wasn't going to leave him there in my home alone because I was fearful of what I would come home to. So, to put his mind at rest, I walked over to the answering machine and replayed the message so we both could hear it. All I wanted to do was put out the fire by any and all means necessary, but from his actions it seemed a little too late. There was absolutely nothing I could do at this point. He was already fuming and the volcano had begun to erupt. I wanted to put his mind at ease, prove to him that I wasn't seeing anyone, and that no one had my phone number. I didn't know what to expect. I was telling him the truth but none of that seemed to matter. Diffuse. That's all I wanted to try and do, but how? What else can I say? What more could I do? The message played." Hello, this is Darryl with the Toyota dealership, can you please give me a call back. You forgot to sign an important piece of paper. I will be in the office until 9 p.m. Please give me a call back when you get this message. Thank you." I looked at my watch and it was 8:57pm. I picked up the phone to try and call him back. I wanted more than anything for him to still be at the dealership so he can diffuse the situation. The phone rang and no answer. I was frantic and was hoping and praying that he would answer this phone. My heart began to beat faster and faster to the point, I could feel it coming through my chest. My palms were sweating. This nervous energy that came over me. It was evident that he was the only person that could diffuse the situation and he had already left the dealership. I thank GOD that was the only message on the answering machine. I thought maybe after hearing the message, he would have picked up on the fact that I drove to the house in a car. Hoping that maybe he would have put two and two together. But NO! It didn't register in his small brain. From what I gathered, he thought that I was probably driving someone else's car. Which was clearly his perception because the next question he asked was, "So what nigga gave you their car, Shaun?" His eyes were so spacy and high from drinking and smoking that he didn't comprehend anything. When he looked at me with those glossy eyes, it was as if he was looking straight through me. All he remembered was hearing a man's voice and assumed the worse like he always did in the past. Each time he was proven wrong, except the times he was actually in the wrong. ADULTERY, LIES, DECEIT! I forgave with accepting blame that I was the cause and the effects of it were his fist. Did my volcano erupt? YES! But I sustained the black and blues more times than enough. After the recording stopped. I cut the machine off and looked at him. I then yelled back." Why are you here in my home listening to my messages and assuming that I am seeing someone? I don't want nobody; I want to be alone!" "I just bought a car for Christ sakes; it was the dealership. Now you need to leave!" By this time I was furious and enraged at this point. I had heard enough. Yet I was scared out of my mind. The physical episodes of abuse left me with a lot of reminders of what I no longer wanted to endure anymore. I wanted to get him out of my home and I clearly didn't want any more issues in front of my children. They had seen enough, and I surely have had enough!

I found myself shouting with anger and clearly I could see that this wasn't going to end smoothly. He was adamant on hearing something different. What if I lied and told him I was dating someone? Would that have changed his mind? Will it have calmed him down, because surely the truth wasn't good enough? The conversation then escalated into a shouting match between us both. He insisted that I was trying to make a liar out of him with the phone call or make him feel stupid for not hearing what he heard. When someone is intoxicated with alcohol and high on drugs, things could become more dangerous and spin out of control very quickly. I dealt with this rage for more than 5 years. Chasing street drugs and alcohol, along with the adultery and fights. I wanted no more of this mental and physical abuse. I had my fair share of busted lips and black eyes, swollen this and that. I tried to reassure him that what he heard was not a boyfriend but a salesperson, but he didn't want to hear that. He even insinuated that the car I was driving was my dad's. Nothing I said was registering to him, absolutely nothing! The last words I heard out of his mouth were, "Bitch if I can't have you, then no fucking body will!" "Bitch, you think I'm stupid or something!" "You dumb ass bitch!" Those were the last words I clearly remember hearing before I was hit with a fist to my face. The first hit to my mouth and then I saw blood. I tried to block his punches, but he was much stronger than I. His rage was overpowering, and he had spun completely out of control at this point. I fell to the floor. He kept punching me in my face while he had me pinned down to the bed. I tried my best to swing back while kicking to get him off of me. All I remember seeing was blood all over the bed, my shirt, and my hands. I began to scream and cry loudly but not realizing that the kids were the only ones in the house that could hear me. The louder I screamed, the lower my vocal cords belted with words and cries for help. It was as if I was crying and yelling in silence. My words had no volume. My ears became deaf in all of the madness. I heard the kids crying upstairs but I couldn't get to them, I became trapped in that room. Trapped with an uncontrolled monster. Trapped like I had been for years with no escape route or plan. As I staggered up off the floor the last punch came to the side of my right ear, and that's when I felt dizzy, dropping on my knees, yet again to the floor. The ringing in my ear from the impact was a pinging in my brain. The pain was excruciating. I faintly heard the echoes of his raging voice and the children screaming and crying. It was as if, I got hit with a bell. The sharp pain inside my head was far too excruciating to bear. I managed to get him up off me and I ran towards the room door leading to the living room, all to find it was locked. My bedroom had two doors on each side. One entrance lead to the living room and the other side led to the kitchen. My only choice at this point was to try and stop him by throwing things at him to hit him hoping to knock him off balance. I needed to try and get out of the room and find safety. He stumbled and fell on the bed, and that's was my chance to make a dash to the other side of the room where there was a door that led to the kitchen area. As I opened the door, I heard him cursing and yelling. I turned around all to see him lift the TV up and throw it at me. I used my right hand to block the TV from hitting my head but my fingers caught the edge of it. With enough force, I was able to hit the TV just enough to redirect the impact away from my head and get out of harm's way. I ran as fast as I could out of the room through the kitchen to safety. I was in so much pain. Unimaginable pain. I got free. I ran out the back sliding door over to my neighbor's yard, all to see that the lights were off. I continued to run, banging on doors, hoping someone would open their door and save me. There was blood everywhere. I had blood dripping down my face, mouth, and hands. I clearly didn't know what was bleeding and I was too scared to find out. Finally, one of my neighbor's lights was on. I had so much blood coming down in my eyes I couldn't tell whose house I was at. Thank GOD! I banged and banged on the door. As she opened the door, I collapsed inside the entryway, begging for help. "Please, you gotta help me. Call the police!" I screamed. Not realizing that it was Evelyn's house I had made it to. I was covered in so much blood that she was assumed I had been shot. I begged her to call the police and to call my dad who lived less than 5 minutes from my house. I let her know that I ran out, but the kids were still inside. They were upstairs in their bedrooms. Not for one moment did I ever think he would do anything to the children. Oftentimes, an abuser will harm those closest to you or even those closest to themselves, whichever gives them vengeful satisfaction but I knew he wouldn't harm the kids. I begged Evelyn to go to the house and check on my babies for me but she was too frightened to go. So she asked her husband to go and grab the kids and ensure they were safe until the police came. He ran down to my house and called her from the entryway of my front door. He said "the door was wide open and he could hear the kids were crying upstairs." He quickly went upstairs to get the kids and calm them down. He reassured the kids that I was ok. I could hear the sirens from the police and ambulance cars speeding up the street. Evelyn tried to clean me up as best she could before the paramedics got there. My head was spinning, and I couldn't hear out of my right ear. My body ached as if I had been ran over by a truck. I was in so much pain. She wrapped my hand in a towel and asked me not to open it until I got to the hospital. My mouth was swollen. I couldn't close it because my lip was busted and my gums was bleeding so bad. She asked me to open my mouth so she could take a look to see where all the blood was actually coming from and that's when she saw that I was also missing my front tooth. This motherfucker knocked my damn tooth out! Are you fucking serious? I tried to get up to look in the hallway mirror but I was in too much pain to move. I couldn't believe what Evelyn was telling me. I then asked her to give me a small mirror so I can see for myself. As she handed me a mirror from it to me, I couldn't believe the horror of what was done to me. I broke down in disbelief. Evelyn asked me to come sit down so she could see what else was wrong and give a clear picture to the police from what little she knew. I had a gash a few centimeters long above my right eyebrow which would require stitches to close. Blood was running down my face coming from that open gash. I asked her to walk with me to my house to see my kids, but she insisted that they not see me this way. Instead, we walked over to the back of the ambulance where my dad was standing there with such anger and rage inside him. All he wanted to do was find him but to no avail, he had left the scene and was nowhere to be found. I fell in his arms and cried uncontrollably. I tried to talk but I was in so much pain at the time, my mouth and lips wouldn't move. I could barely see out of my right eye and my dad could bare to look at what all was done to me. He rode with the police to search for him after I gave them a description but no sight of him anywhere. Evelyn's husband said the kids were safe, they were just scared, and they would watch them while I went to the hospital to get checked out. My dad opted to stay at the house while I was gone just in case he came back. Most abusers sometimes come back to the scene when they feel the coast is clear. The assailants are never far away from the scene of a crime especially when they feel their business is unfinished. They are just far enough to not be seen or get caught, but they are always watching!

I arrived at the hospital and was immediately taken back to triage in the Emergency Room. There was a domestic violence counselor that came in to talk with me after the nurse did her initial assessment and vitals. It was the hospital standard protocol with cases like mines, whereby a counselor assessed the needs of the victim. The nurse re-entered the room to complete her assessment prior to the doctor consult. The nurse gently unwrapped the towel that Evelyn had put on my wounds and was taken aback with silence and could only offer words of comfort after what she has seen. She rewrapped my hand in the towel to soak up the bleeding and advised me to apply pressure to slow down the blood loss. The pain was too painful to the touch that it began throbbing even more. I couldn't bear to look so I turned my head in the other direction. The police officer stood outside of the door waiting for her to finish with her initial examination so he could come inside and speak with me to do his report. He insisted that I also get a stay away order as protocol of protection. Who would have thought a good day would get so bad. All I wanted was to enjoy the day with my kids, take them out and spend some quality time with them. We were finally at a place of peace in our life. I walked away from the abuse that spanned for years. I had had enough and we suffered in silence for far too long. Why wasn't that enough for us both! I grew tired of going to work with bruises and swollen faces and calling out because of them. Covering up gashes with makeup. Hiding from friends and family for weeks until I healed. Most importantly, lying to the kids by telling them everything will be ok when I knew it wouldn't be until we was free. I was not ok even though I told them I was. I was dying inside. I had gained so much weight from depression. I had gained up to 320 lbs. and wore a size 26 in women's clothes. I truly, truly, didn't feel good about myself in this relationship. I let myself go. All lies needed to stop before someone loses their life. Tonight could have been me!

I was finally at a place where wanting better was the priority. I wanted out and my kids deserved better than this. I knew I deserved better than this! The devil came back to play and this time I didn't let him in. I fought back the best I could. I may have lost the fight but I won the battle. The battle to leave a toxic environment. The battle to want better. After the nurse cleaned me up a bit and left the room, I wanted to see me! I wanted to see what was done to me. I managed to get up from the table and walk over to the mirror. My face. Disfigured. Swollen. The damage done to my face this time was worse than ever before. I couldn't stand to look at me in the mirror. My eyes were swollen, and I had a large gash above my right eyebrow, in which, the nurse said measured about a 2 inch gap right over the eyelid. I opened my mouth and saw that my front tooth was missing. All I could do was cry. I broke down in tears and couldn't stop crying. How could he have done this to me? I didn't deserve this at all! I had no contact with him. No arguments. No fights. I completely walked away because the kids and I needed that. We needed a fresh start. We needed a break. There was no other man that I was seeking but GOD himself. I made HIS place in our lives first and foremost. I thought I finally got it right. I thought I had it all figured out. I was happy being by myself, just me and my kids, and we were finally at a place where we could laugh and grow in a completely uncomplicated world where we wouldn't be harmed; where we wouldn't cry or have fears. Their dad died years ago. It was my duty as mom to protect them and keep them from harm, yet I couldn't even protect myself. He prepared me for moments like this. This is why he made me strong and fearless. Yet I failed his lessons. I failed me! To be a sole provider in case of absence. He prepared me to not fear, so where was it when I needed to be the most? Why and how did I lose it? I was fearful and scared of my attacker. Why? My primary focus was to try and give my children the best that I could single handedly. I thought that was enough when folks would want you to do better, be better, but not with him. My children finally had a place to call home, their home! To see them playing freely in the backyard or up in their bedrooms, running through the house, playing in the basement was joyous. They didn't have to worry about neighbors telling them to be quiet due to the tapping of their feet running through the apartment over their heads. They didn't have to worry about rodents and mice crawling around. They had freedom to be kids! Now I'm battered and beaten all over again. I'm broken into pieces after I pieced my life together from being shattered and broken. I'm ugly all over again! Our home, this home, now has a mark of pain that followed us from the last. Reminders of where we just were is what I wanted and tried my best to avoid. I don't know how I can ever change that. EVER!

As the nurse entered the room, she began to console me and talk to me as she too had been through some of the same experiences. She spoke about her personal journey to break free even though it took her a long time, but she did it. She went into hiding, but felt that I was stronger than she was. I wanted him to face me because I didn't want to show fear in the eyes of my enemy. I know I will rise again, but when? How long will it take me this time? This ordeal has made me believe that no matter what, I will always be found! I will forever be broken. No matter what, in my heart I will always be on the run. Running from the truth with lies. Running from the secrets and regrets. No matter what I will have some fears. I don't want self-pity or people feeling sorry for me. My friends would always say to me that I am this hopeless romantic and live in a bubble when it comes to love and its expectations. I just want to be loved because that's what I give. Why is it so hard for people to show love, true love without expectation? Why do they think that hurting is an example of love? She too had no answer for me.

The nurse told me that my wounds were going to require a few stitches above my eye to close the gash. She then asked me to extend my hand so she could unwrap the towel that had been used as the anchor. I couldn't bear to look at my hand. She said, "OMG!" "Half your finger is split in half." I screamed and screamed. "Please put it back together, please." She asked me to stay calm and that she was going to get the doctor to come take a look at it. She immediately wrapped it back in the towel and asked me to hold my arm upright to redirect the blood flow as much as possible. I just couldn't get my bearings to stop crying. Things got bad with us but never this bad. I have had plenty of busted lips and swollen faces but never missing any parts of me or even a tooth for that matter. I will forever look in the mirror and be reminded of what was done to me. The doctor came in and began his assessment before treatment. He first looked at the gash on my head and asked the nurse to prep for stitching. He said, "Let's deal with what's in front of us first, ok?" I sobbed and replied, "Ok." The stitching on my eye was done first and my finger second. He wanted to take it one step at a time. I was beyond hurt and forgiveness wasn't an option for me. I didn't want any communication ever again with him of any kind. There were no more options left for me. My heart was beyond shattered and numb. The doctor asked me to unwrap the towel so he could see what can be done to save it. He asked me to look at him as he explained what he could do. My pinky finger on the right hand had been severed in half. The inside tissue was open and sitting outside of the skin. It was split in half like a banana. My adrenaline was running so high that I didn't even feel the pain. It wasn't until I calmed down when the pain became noticeable and quite unbearable. When the TV was thrown, I used my right hand to block it from hitting me in the head. The tissue inside of the skin was exposed and nerves were damaged beyond repair due to the impact. He said he could sew it back together and put the dead tissue inside the skin, but I will never be able to feel completely with this finger again. The other option would be to sever the rest of what's left of the finger and create a nub on the end. WAIT! Do you mean I will walk around with the loss of a finger? I am not going to be reminded anymore of this nightmare with a finger missing too. I begged him to keep my finger together. I was already broken inside and must find a way to repair my front tooth before I can ever be seen in public. This was mental torture for me. I will never be the same! Having to be reminded of this nightmare is what I didn't want to live with for the rest of my life but again, GOD gave us memories. No matter how much I wanted to forget this day, it would be merely impossible. So the thing is to try and ensure that I am not reminded of this day for the rest of my life. I must learn how to cope with what has happened to me the best way I know how. With the nurse's assistance, they began to sew my finger back together. I received my discharge papers and the police officer took me back home. All I wanted most in this world at this very moment was to hug my children and make sure they were ok. They were more concerned about me rather than I concerned about them. That's how they always were during past altercations. They were strong kids, but my primary focus was protecting them from harm unlike what all I had endured. Even though I didn't do a good job with protecting myself, I made sure they were always ok. Physically they were ok, but the mental scars will last a lifetime. Look at how I am presenting myself to them. Another incident that they had to witness and go through at the hands of an abuser. He was someone that they looked up to and had been in their lives for a long time. What if the things they saw effected them and their future relationships? This is not the example I wanted to set for my children. I tried to protect them from that, but now I must try and teach them the right way of how they should give and receive love. I feel I let them down! I let myself down! It's all my fault for choosing and dealing with this for so long. I wasn't prepared like I thought I was all these years. Mental preparedness is the biggest piece of overcoming situational experiences. It will give you a sense of direction. I gave him too much control in the past. Control over me and control over my life. In this relationship, I became too comfortable, complacent and accepted the wrong things to fall in love with. I substituted the real for the fake, even when I knew it was not right. I hoped for change but continued to live in a fairytale bubble hoping that things will get better with time. They say time heals all wounds. But how much time will it take!

When I got home from the hospital, my dad was there waiting while the kids were upstairs in their beds. I reassured him that I will be ok. He said that he didn't think he would come back to the house but if I needed him to call. After he left, I made sure the kids were ok and settled in bed. They appeared to not be asleep but laying quietly and motionless. They didn't really know what to say but seeing my face back at home was enough. I began checking all windows and doors and completely locking the house down after my dad left. I allowed them to see me in all my darkness. I never hid my scars from them not one time. Maybe I should have. I always used those moments as teachable moments, but what can you tell a 6 year old or even a 5 year old about life and what to and not to expect while living in its moments. How can I make them understand when they are constantly witnessing this kind of madness? They didn't have questions but wanted to ensure that he wouldn't come back to the house. I assured them that we were safe. I sat up with them until they all fell off to sleep, then I went downstairs to my bedroom to assess the damage. I stood in the middle of the bedroom, all to see blood splattered everywhere, holes in the walls, and my TV laying on the floor cracked and shattered. It was a complete mess. The view shattered me, but what was crying going to solve at this point. I was in too much pain to even bend over to lift anything. All I wanted to do was ensure that he wouldn't reappear. I needed to ensure that the kids and I would be safe for the night. Even if it meant I had to come face to face with the devil again himself and give my life to save my babies, I was up for the challenge. As I sat downstairs by the window, my son comes downstairs and hops on my lap. He was barely 3 years old at the time, but he sensed mommy was hurt. He couldn't sleep and was frightened. As he sat on my lap, he hugged me and began patting the back of my shoulder as to say, it will be ok! I began to cry with him in my arms and he lifted his head up and said, "Stop crying mommy, don't cry mommy!" He then wiped my tears and laid his head down on my shoulder and fell off to sleep in my arms. That was GOD sending his angel down to tell me everything was going to be ok and there was no need for tears! I was still alive to see another day and those days from now on will shine brighter than the days before.

Dear Heavenly Father,

We have been suffocating for years in this madness that we dwell in. All we want most in the world is for our lungs to open so that we can breathe again. All we want is to breathe again, Heavenly Father. We want to inhale the air and expand. Instead, we are continuing to suffocate in sadness. Take us to the light, so that we can see what a bright future we have walking hand in hand with you. It is you that we seek, Father GOD. We ask for your hand as our covenant to walk in the footprints of the sand. We will continue to follow your walk into the heavenly skies above. We honor you and give you praise. In Jesus Name, we pray. **AMEN**

Six: Wake Up Call

Day Two and Forever:

The night was long, and I hadn't had the strength to clean up a thing. I was fearful that he would return. I put my son to bed once he fell asleep in my arms and proceeded downstairs to ensure that every lock was locked, and every door was bolted shut. I sat up quietly in the living room looking out the window until I too fell off to sleep. I didn't care what happened at this point, just as long as we were no longer in danger and out of harm's way. I couldn't stand to go back in the bathroom or even walk past the mirror. The horror of what I looked like was too much for me to bear. Disfigured was the best word I could describe my face, and it hurt me to the core to have my children see me this way! There were no other choices and walking away was the only option at the end of the day. It wasn't just about me, but about us. My children and I and their future as loving people who will someday have a family of their own. I sat cold inside. Numb. I had nothing left. It was at that moment, I felt I had nothing left inside of me but pain.

I woke up to sounds of sirens and I immediately became scared after what I just endured. I couldn't close my eyes again. The thought of what happened hours ago literally had me watching all windows and doors without wanting to close my eyes. I kept peeking outside around the Ever-bush tree that stood in front of my front porch steps as I sat in the view of the window. Ensuring that he was no longer on my property or at my door. Still so surreal in the moment. I sat with rage and anger all over again. At every impulse, my face and hand began to ache with such pain and the fact that I had a missing tooth, made me even angrier. How can any man ever want me again? How can I walk around disfigured and everyone will see that I was abused? How can I ever look my kids in the eye and know they understand that Mommy tried, and yet she still couldn't escape the past? What was I to teach them going forward? How can I go to work, again, looking like this? With all these bruises and missing body parts, stitches, and bandages. What mess has become of me? All these questions continued to run through my mind. Questions I didn't have answers to. Questions after questions and I had not one god-damn answer to them. NOT ONE!

The shame I felt after being told so many times to walk away, yet I forgave and gave in to the madness. The make-up moments. Every relationship has them and mines sure as hell was no different from any other. Whether it's mental or physical. Someone has said something that hurt the matters of the heart at one point or another. It may not have been constant but one time of happening is enough to cause a lifetime of pain. So, I forgave all the black eyes, swollen faces, and busted lips. I forgave with all the stupid excuses and blames for things being my fault when truly it wasn't. I forgave thinking things would change or get better. I forgave assuming that abuse was love and that was the only way to show it. I forgave because I didn't know my self-worth. I forgave for fear of being alone and being told that no one would want a woman with all these kids. So, I stayed and accepted the things I thought I could change, and I knew was wrong! I made excuses for the bad habits that lead to the abuse. I consumed it the many times I allowed others to see me raw and in pain. I was so emotionally wrecked that there were times I went to work and forgot to wear my makeup. I was exposed! The abuse at the hands of an attacker was exposed! No more hiding. No more lying. No more covering up. The truth is out and I must now face my reality. All I thought about was that my bills needed to be paid and my kids needed to eat. Barely able to walk, so I continued to walk in pain. The times I walked miles to find him barefoot and pregnant, and penniless, when I didn't hear from him for days at a time. Thinking I could save him from the ways of the worldly sins and the foolishness thereof. When love finally came home, so did the punches. They too said we are home and I welcomed them. The pain I endured daily. The only person who could save me, was me. Could I be saved? Did I want to be rescued? All I knew was that one day, it will end. At least I thought it would when I walked away this one last time.

Exhausted to say the least. I finally dozed off to sleep and the morning came shining brightly through the windows. It was as if GOD said, "I'm here and you are safe with me." I woke up and dropped the kids off at the bus stop and daycare. I grabbed the phone to call my supervisor to let him know I couldn't make it in for a few days. He was all too familiar with my battery incidents over the years. He was always concerned for me. "Are you alright, this time? He hit you again, didn't he?" I replied, "Yes, and this time it was bad." As I spoke, I began to weep. He begged me to stop crying and listen to him as he spoke. "You know I got your back always, but enough is enough. I know you tried this time, but I think this time you need to get the law involved." He paused and then continued to speak. "This nigga ain't shit, because any fool who puts his hand on a woman is a coward. And you can tell him I said it!" He was angry but he has always been there for me. I knew he meant what he said. He knew just how much I needed my job and how much I loved my kids. He always told me that I reminded him of his mother raising him and his siblings and the hardships she too endured. He wished this on no woman and was a man who didn't tolerate abuse of any kind. After I explained to him what happened, all he wanted to do was get me to a dentist to fix my tooth. He gave me a number to the local dentist, someone he knew personally and would take good care of me. He told that me to contact him right away and that he would fit me in today. He also gave me a week off to get myself together and get the law involved. I was ever so grateful for his support and understanding. I didn't have any friends that I could lean on except my neighbors when I needed them to look after the kids while I was ran late from work or needed to run errands.

After we talked, I called the dentist and sure enough he fit me in for an evening appointment, preferably the last one of the day. Thank GOD, I can get my tooth fixed today. I had a few hours before the kids got home from school and I needed to start the clean-up. I didn't want them to come home to the mess and be reminded of what happened. There were holes in the walls and blood all over the carpet and floor. The room was a complete wreck. Where do I begin and I needed help. I called our neighborhood handyman, who usually cuts the grass every two weeks along with doing minor work around the house, to see if he was free to come do a few repairs. I didn't go into any details at that time nor did I want to bother my dad with the aftermath. I just wanted to get things fixed and allow the healing to begin. I removed all the broken things and cleared the trash so that the repairs could begin and things that I kept was moved to an empty room on the other side of the house. I didn't want to sleep in that room again and be reminded of what had happened.

After I moved the furniture, it was time for me to go and get the kids. I had enough time to take them to their grand-parent's house for a little while, while I go to the dentist to get my tooth fixed. I asked the dentist to make me the last appointment of the day, if it was possible. He said naturally his walk-ins would be last anyway. That truly subsided my anxiety of anyone seeing me like this. I already felt embarrassed and was much relieved that he could fit me in so quickly.

By the time I arrived for my appointment, my supervisor had already spoken to him regarding my visit. He asked me to sit in the back office until he was ready for me. He was a big man in stature, and this was a family-owned dental office. His daughters worked there as his clinical assistants and admin personnel. It was a very family-oriented yet professional office. He too was a father who can understand having daughters in his life. After he examined my tooth space, he sat down in the chair beside me. He spoke with sternness. "Look at me, "He said, "I can tell by these bruises and swelling that someone did you no good, am I right?" When he spoke, I didn't realize that he could tell I had bruises. I tried my best to cover up these scars with makeup. A normal routine I had thought I mastered for years. You can fool some of them sometimes but not all of them all the time. That was a saying I grew up with from my elders and it surely fit the equation in my adult life. So true! He was not fooled at all. He turned the mirror my way and I noticed that as he was working on my tooth, my make-up wore off. I was exposed! Ashamed! Embarrassed! He knows I had been beaten. I couldn't look him in the eye. I turned away as if I was his child getting ready to be scolded for doing something bad. He repeated himself. "Look at me!" The innocence of my inner child-like behavior overtook my emotions of being an adult. It was as if a father was scolding his child. I could only imagine how my own father felt that very night. I looked into his piercing eyes and said, "That's correct sir. I had gotten out of relationship almost 2 months ago, and he came back for me." He then paused and bowed his head. As he continued to work on fixing my tooth, he kept saying, "Let's make you whole again, shall we." He repeated that phrase to himself as he continued working to repair the damage of another man's fist. He asked no further questions or made no other comment as his focus was on his goal of making me whole again. It was at this moment, I had to realize that I couldn't change what had happened, wished it was different, but I will forever being scarred mentally and physically for life. Every day I look in the mirror, all I will forever see is a part of me missing and replaced, but never whole again. This wasn't how GOD made me to be. My image was ruined, and I will have to explain to everyone that I give a smile to, why a part of me is missing. Everyone will know, I was beaten or in some sort of altercation. Father GOD why did this happen to me? WHY!

As he finished up and gave me a temporary tooth, he showed me the mirror. He said that my permanent tooth will not be ready for another 4 to 6 weeks and this one should hold until it comes in. As I looked in the mirror, all I could see was shattered dreams of imperfections! My smile was not beautiful but at least there wasn't an empty space in my mouth, just in my heart! I walked to the front to check-out and his daughter just looked at me. She asked me if she could give me a hug. I obliged and began to weep uncontrollably. It was at that moment, that I realized I wasn't alone. I was uncovered yet scarred to death! I needed to allow healing to begin, but how do I start and where do I begin. Some-way, some-how, the clean-up must now begin.

As I approached my home, the handyman was there at the house to assist me with repairing the damage. The holes were repaired, the locks were changed, ADT was contacted for an alarm system to be put on the house, but most importantly, the screen door was added to the front with entry key. I began creating a sense of security for the kids and I, AND the front door security lock was the start. There biggest fear was that he would come back, and I had to do all I could to ensure them that our house was safe again. Safe for us to live in and even safer for them in my absence. I received a call from the police officer who came to the house and escorted me to and from the hospital. He asked me to come and join their police enforcement self-defense classes that were given to battered women by the police department. OK! The thought that I am classified as a battered women was a real wake-up for me. The realization that I fell into that category shook me to the core. For years I endured. For years I was in a bad relationship without knowing the ending would turn out like this. This took me to a place that I never thought I would be. I didn't have to go to the mirror for realization, the world, and the existence thereof, came to me. That's the "slap in your face" moment that has begun to haunt me now and forever. I attended the classes and found the fight in me that I had lost. The will to no longer be the victim of violent relationships and circumstances. The will to teach my children what not to accept and to know that there are options. Lastly, I pressed charges and obtained a stay away order for a year! I walked away after years of the abusive relationship and its toxicity. After years of excuses and years of accepting the life of lies, I finally walked away and never looked back with no regrets. The road to recovery was long but the car only carried my children, and I wasn't picking up any passengers along the way!

I never spoke to him about what and all he did to me. He never stuck around that night to see the damage. It took him 12 years to apologize, and though it did come, I accepted it with grace but through my faith in GOD, I forgave him before, during, and after the damage was done. Of course, I wished I could have forgotten, however, because we are blessed with memories, though tragic, the pain has long subsided! To this day, he never knew and now 26 years later, he still don't know! In 2019, at the strike of COVID, I was home eating dinner, and that tooth broke loose and came out. OMG! 26 years later I had to relive that day all over again. I jumped up and ran to the bathroom, all to see the ugliness of what he created in me. I tried to put the tooth back in my mouth but it kept falling out. I began to cry and cry because I didn't wasn't to relive this nightmare. The fear of that night came rushing through my soul, through my gut and more than anything, I wanted to get angry. A nightmare that I thought I was over and healed from. A nightmare that haunted me for years and although I had given that to GOD and forgave, I wanted to take those buried words of: "I accept your apology", and "I forgive you"… I wanted to take those words back. GOD you didn't prepare me for this part. This tooth was supposed to be in forever, but instead it showed up again. I clearly remember the dentist office that put the tooth in, so I googled the office location and dentist and called them immediately. When I called them, the answering machine picked up, however, the name of the dentist office was different. I sat and thought what I could do to seal my tooth in the meantime on my own. I couldn't go out looking like this in front of people, let alone, my boyfriend. I forgot about him! What will he think? For years past, my dentist office soon closed due to COVID and didn't reopen for 2.5 years later. During this time, I continue to seal my tooth with cement adhesive that I obtained off Amazon and that was my saving grace along with money. In 2023, I became whole again. I ensured that this time, my teeth are permanent and my smile is as bright as ever. My self-confidence is so high that I am no longer torn. I smile with grace and live with a purpose unbothered and unharmed. My first ever photoshoot with this smile was taken 3/09/2023 and for the first time in over 30 years, I love who I see in the mirror, scarred and all!!!

<u>THROUGH HIS STRIPES WE ARE HEALED! ISAIAH 53:5</u>

Sept: The Unborn Cumpany We Keep

We all lose things gracing this precious earth and walking through our own lifetime. Some things can be controlled or uncontrolled, intentional or accidental, but premeditated acts have effects we don't prepare ourselves for, yet only GOD knows why things happen the way they do. Do we question the "Why's?" We are taught to never question our parents or GODs intentions, but there were times in my life that it crossed my mind. I walked this precious earth assuming that this was HIS plan for me. SUFFERING! HURT! PAIN! RAGE! UNLOVED!

Choosing love by accepting what I thought was love, is why I felt punished. I could never do right or make the right choices according to other peoples rule book. I wasn't good enough and always thought to take the wrong path in life, as they thought of me. They didn't have a problem with saying it either. The older I got, the more I realized and was told from a wise woman that, "the more they talk about you, the more you are doing right!" When you aren't shown things in life, you tend to go searching for the void unfilled. Yearning for the feeling of it. Yearning for the smell of it. Yearning for the touch of it. No matter where or how you got it, but as long as you got it! Even if it meant costing you in the end. So let's chat about the elephant in the room. ME. As they say, elephants live the longest anyway.

I had been single for a few years, the love of being alone was ideal to me. Nobody to blame but me. I cherished my peace of mind and my home was my serenity safe haven. The introduction to date again was a thought always retained but, I wasn't interested in. My friends insisted I get out and meet. I wasn't the kind of person who randomly date people and the thought of going from person to person was not lady-like. Although I loved being settled in one relationship at a time and once it was over, I cleansed for however long it took: mentally and physically. I would spiritually know when I was ready and until then I remained content within my sacred space. Celibate for a lack of better words. After my past relationships ended, my primary focus was my children and my well-being. We were scarred in such a way, that we needed to breathe again. I know they wanted happiness for me, but I felt I was already happy without a companion. You never know what good things could come out of it, especially if there's truth! Truth and trust from both parties that is. Going into situations blindly assuming that others have your best interest at heart, has been very disheartening to say the least. We think of friendship as: "I got your back, you got mines!", "my confidant", "and My support system!" "My protector!" We hold true to those values and expect the same in return. But, what happens when we don't receive the return and find out the friendship isn't genuine but operates with jealousy and malice. GOD teaches us to forgive thy brethren, but what he doesn't mention is that we will never be able to forget. Trajectory doesn't allow us to forget. HE gives us memories for a reason: everlasting thoughts we wish we could erase or start over, especially after we learn the fate of actions intended. I forgave you all, but don't think for one second I forgot how it all went down!

Ladies night and I got a call from one of my friends to go to a house party of someone she knows really well. I was not the partying type nor did I drink alcohol or ever did drugs. I lived to age gracefully as my grandmother taught me to do. My life was all about work, school, and my babies. But nonetheless, I felt the need to go out and be a safe driver for the night. All my friends and associates drank or did some type of drug, while a few did both. Normalcy was the true definition. They kept it real! But no one did anything harmful besides smoking weed. I was considered the one that could get everybody home safely after their night out of having fun. Everyone need a safety net, I guess I was that one.

We pulled up to this housing development where there were rows of parked cars and lots of people outside playing loud music. We went inside to where my friend greeted everyone. I never knew she knew so many people. I followed her upstairs and found me a spot in a corner all by myself, right by the speakers, but with a view near the exit door should anything pop off, I could make a clean dash out of there. I wasn't by far outgoing and crowds of unknown people wasn't my thing, however, the atmosphere was ok. Just your regular kind of house party vibe going on. Lots of laughter, dancing, drinking and smoking going on. Observation is key in foreign territories. I sat enjoying the music, again I was in my happy space. I love music of all kinds, so I sort of tuned out the audience and channeled my energy on my inner self for that moment. I closed my eyes and allowed the music to take me to a place of resolve. A place of laughter, fun, and smiles. My grandmother would always walk with a beat of music in her soul. You could catch her at the stove singing and dancing as she cooked our meals. She said music keeps you living beyond your years. I followed her footsteps because she practiced what she preached. She lived on to be 98 years young. The room soon was filled with this smoke cloud that I couldn't escape unless I went outside. I opened my eyes, got up to stand and became noticeably dizzy from inhaling the essence of marijuana smoke. They call it "contact smoking!" They say second hand smoke is worse than being a smoker yourself. I guess for me, I caught a case of the "get highs." I have never smoked anything and wasn't about to start now. I immediately went out to the deck for some fresh air and to clear my lungs. It was summertime and the night air smelled of oak trees while the full moon lit up the night sky. The summer nights were beautiful especially if you can see the sun set in the evenings. Well, right now the only thing that mattered was for me to breathe anything except the smell of weed.

As I sat alone on the deck looking up at the night sky, I heard a voice ask me if I was ok. I quickly turned around and there stood a handsome, clean-shaved, man. Stocky build with a bald head. He was my type of man. I couldn't help but lock eyes with him continuously throughout the evening because he was the one who supplied what was making everyone happy while dancing. The weed. I didn't see him drink or smoke any of the drugs, which was a plus for me, while everyone else seemed to be doing just the opposite. I obliged him with a reply, "Yes, I'm ok. Just getting some air." " It is too much smoke in there for me and I don't do drugs of any kind, so I am out here until my friend is ready to leave." He walked around to the front of me, to where I could see his face and said, "Ok, but if you need anything let me know!" My heart began to race after I had a good look at his face. For that very split second, my mind was placed in the bedroom. I quickly looked away from him to gather my thoughts back to reality. He was very handsome, clean shaved and gorgeous build. I immediately replied to him and asked if he had a bottle of water. He said "Yes, I will be right back." After receiving the water, we talked a little while longer before exchanging numbers.

As the months and days went by, we grew closer. My intentions was never to rush into anything and I was determined more than ever on taking things slow while trying to get to know this person on my terms. I worked a lot and we only saw each other two times a week but talked daily. Things were going quite well and I didn't allow this friendship to deviate my daily activities and lifestyle. Again, my safe space was necessary and very important for my own healing. Work was always the grind that ensured that I didn't have to ask anyone for anything. The strength in me to provide for my children's needs was my centerpiece. I pushed forward no matter what the circumstance. Work was also my personal appreciation to life: my "I love you" in silence, my gratefulness. Work was the "Yes" to all the "No's" I received in life. Work was my "Thank You!" Work was my savior from self-harm and destruction. Work was my focus!

Although it was hard for me to let anyone in my safe space, I allowed him to enter. Maybe I shouldn't have. Maybe the timing was not right. Maybe I just wasn't ready for anything, but I forced myself to be ready for everything. I came home from work this night exhausted, tired as usual, but a hard day's work pays off in the end. I called him when I got in, which was our usual to end the days. His behavior had changed and he seemed to be a little agitated and irate. I didn't think anything of it at first, but assumed that he just had a bad day. He often times would vent about his living arrangement, so I assumed that that was the issue. But this night was a little different. He seemed more out of sorts than his normal behavior. When I asked him what was going on, he couldn't express his words to me. The more frustrated he became, the more agitated I got, but, I didn't push his buttons. You never know a person's limitations and what they may do if pushed to the edge. All I wanted to do was try and keep the peace between us as much as possible. We had only had been dating for six months and I wanted to give him his space that allowed him time to calm down and get his-self together. His attitude grew worse the more we talked so I immediately ended the call and entertained my own inner peace. His burden was not mines to carry. That shit ages you and why should I allow myself to get stressed out over someone else's problems. My mother always told me to not carry someone's problems that don't have my name on it! So that is what I live by.

We hadn't spoken for over a week. I thought that he would at least give me a call and communicate. Prior to this drama, we always spoke daily, however, due to the lack of communication, space was ok but necessary. I had been under the weather that week and I finally gave in and called him to see if maybe he too was sick. He said that he was for a few days but shook it off as a 24 hour virus. He assumed that maybe it was something he had eaten because he was very nauseated but he felt better. I asked him if he had a runny nose because he kept sniffing and he said no, he is just getting over things. Well needless to say, I was down for the count and had taken off work the entire week. I scheduled an appointment with my doctor to get some antibiotics and he wanted to go with me. He said he had missed me a lot and he felt we needed to talk and make amends for his behavior. I honestly wanted to see him, but I didn't want to entertain any drama.

As I sat with him at the doctor's office, however, the wait was so long that I opted to go home. I couldn't wait any longer. I informed the receptionist that I was going to reschedule. My head started spinning, I was dizzy and everyone in the doctor's office was sick. Fuck! I hated falling ill and having to take off work. I just wanted to get out of there. There also was a stench in the air that made me sick to my stomach. He helped me to the car and decided to drive us home. He said he felt bad that I was sick but he kept making jokes to bring light to the situation. I noticed him wiping his nose quite often although he said it wasn't running and he was over his cold, I kind of felt like he too was still sick but just didn't want to tell me. Men never want to claim any illness and they are the biggest punks when it comes to needles. That's probably why he wanted us to leave the doctor's office. As we were riding home, we decided to stop by the dollar store to grab some household things. He said he wanted to get some soup and tissue and things to help take care of me tonight. I liked that idea a lot. He suggested we stay at his place with his family instead of me being home alone. So we stopped by my house grab some clothes before heading to his house. A sense of calm came over me and it felt good to have someone look after me for once. I felt comfortable in his presence. Everyone seems to think that I never needed anything or anyone to do for me, but that clearly was not the case. I was tired of being told "NO", so I learned to lean on myself. My kids was with their grandparents at the time so I had alone time. Some me time!

We sat up watching movies while he nursed me back to health. He had a gentle, nurturing spirit about himself which ensured me that I was in good hands. I hadn't experienced this in years. I had just gotten out of a marriage but the divorce wasn't yet finalized. It had a lot of good times but towards the end, we became two very distant people. From that point on, I sheltered myself from anyone and I never allowed closeness. I didn't want to get hurt or be mistreated. Not that I had been in my past but I didn't want to experience it none the less. Besides, relationships in general take a lot out of a person and all I wanted to do was live and be loved in return. Simple right!

His phone rang and he went upstairs to talk. He said he didn't want to interrupt and be loud while I was resting. I didn't mind that because he appeared to not have any skeletons or keep any secrets from me. I didn't feel like he was hiding anything from me at all. IF anything, I was never that open with him about my past either. I was never open with anyone but me! True to oneself was easy. Adaptable. Comforting. Selfish. I expected from others without giving of myself in the same way.

As I sat watching TV, I could overhear him talking loudly out on the deck. I got up and walked towards the back door. His bedroom was in the basement of the house with the patio right under the deck so I cracked open the door to hear what was making him so angry. I didn't want to ease drop but curiosity got the best of me. What was making him so angry and could this have been what he was so aggravated about last week was what I thought? What was he not telling me? I overheard him talking to what appeared to be a lady about parole and jail time. WAIT. Did I just hear the words parole and jail time? He never told me he was affiliated with jail or even on parole. I had to listen for more before jumping to my own conclusions. His family member came out on the balcony and told him to stop yelling for fear that others would hear him. I assumed she meant me, because I was the only other person in the house. I stood there listening even more. He was angry because the lady on the phone informed him that he missed his meeting to give urine and was in jeopardy of going back to jail. He was explaining to his family that he didn't know of the appointment and the letter he received didn't state any of the fact. He said he put the letter in his nightstand drawer. While they continue to engage in heavy conversation, I ran to the nightstand drawer to see if the letter was there and what was it all about. I found it and was in total shock of what I was reading about him. I didn't believe for once that he would keep secrets from me or no secrets like this. Why did he keep things from me and who is this person that I am with? Talk about a blow to my heart. All I wanted to do was run out of there and go the hell home. Barricade myself in my home and never come out. I heard him come in off the deck and start walking towards the basement door. I quickly put the letter back and jumped back on the bed and under the covers. I was trembling but had to play the part without him suspecting anything. At this point, I was stuck there with this maniac for the night. Wondering should I sneak off when he goes to sleep or leave in the morning and never come back. I didn't know what was safer for me. All I knew was that I had to get out of there and away from him.

As he made his way back to the bedroom, I calmly asked him if everything was ok. He said yeah, it was someone he knew and that they called him tripping. WAIT! Did this nigga just lie to me? No he tripping if he think that was OK. So let me ask again. "Is everything ok? Do you want to talk about it?" He said not really. He tried to play things off and that pissed me off even more. But again, I don't know this fool and he got some skeletons that is trying to come the hell out of the closet and play. So let's play. He tried to play things off by joking but he wasn't doing a good job of hiding things from me. After he saw that I wasn't in the playing mood, he pulled out the paper in his drawer. He went to explain that he was locked up for drug possession and attempted murder. He then went to his closet and pulled out some pictures of him in jail. Motherfucking jail pictures. You have got to be kidding me. Did he really think him posing with his homeboys, dapped up, in stripes was fucking cute. REALLY NIGGA! What the fuck is cute about jail pictures? You mean to tell me that I have been laid up with a nigga who been in the pen. Seventeen years he said with a damn smile. Well, give this nigga a lit cigarette to hang out the side of his mouth while he talking shit, for Christ's sake! My mind and head was spinning. How in the hell did I miss the signs with my green-as-grass ass? I am laying up with a penitentiary Type A motherfucker. Ain't this some shit! My mind started racing. Wondering. Thinking. Questions came over me. I asked him how long he was in there. He said he was locked up for 17 years. He had just came home a year ago and that he is on 5 year supervised probation. He must give urines monthly, if not sporadic when they say. I sat there eagerly for his ass to keep on talking, more and more. He then says, "Yeah they can't catch me quick enough on that urine shit." As he starts to laugh, oh girl is steaming at this point. I grew angrier underneath my skin. He said that when he was in, he got really depressed and was sent to the hole a few times for fighting. So when he came home, they put him on meds to decrease the anxiety. He said he is supposed to take the medication twice a day or when necessary. He said he has a doctor that he also sees and that he is supposed to go see another doctor to talk to but he don't feel he needs that. He has been controlling things on his own and his family makes sure he takes his meds. He said being in the hole has kept him from sleeping with the lights off, he have bad dreams of bugs and mice crawling on him, and the smell of urination and feces. OK. So let a bitch digress this shit. Not only am I sitting next to a motherfucker who been in the pen but your ass is crazy as a loony-toon also. All I could do was take a deep breath and find my next move to exit the fuck out of that house. I don't need no crazy ass niggas trying to kill me all because he off his meds. As he was trying to explain the murder and gun charges, I completely zoned out again. It was only a silent echo in my ear and I wasn't up to hearing anymore of this horror story, let alone live in it. I began plotting in my mind about how I could get home safely and distance myself from the foolishness. I wanted more than anything to call that so-called friend of mines and ask her why she didn't inform me of her folks. Why didn't she say anything when she knew we had started dating each other? Like, bitch beware or don't get into this. Something to warn a sister about what I could be facing. Friends. The more I thought, the sicker I got. I jumped up and ran to the bathroom. My stomach was so queasy. I couldn't stop trembling from the fear of this person. A man I don't even know. The thought of being with a killer just sickened me to death and I wanted no parts of it or him.

He came to the bathroom door asked me if I was ok. I informed him that my stomach was sick but I would be fine. He said that he wanted me to ride with him to the store to get something to eat because he grew an appetite. At first I was hesitant but after today's event, I quickly changed my mind. I put on my shoes and coat and we headed out. As we was driving, I wanted to jump the hell out of the moving car and run but I refrained from such thoughts and went along for the ride. He made a joke to try and bring light to the situation by saying how it would be funny if I'm sick because I am pregnant. NOW that shit made a bitch angry all over again. I wanted to ball up my fist and beat this nigga upside his crooked ass mouth for saying that shit. This fool talking trash. The fuck if I am pregnant and it wouldn't be by your ass. That's for damn sure. You crazy motherfucker. These thoughts came across my mind so quickly that I almost slipped the words out of my mouth. Instead I said calmly, "please don't say such a thing, besides, my tubes are tied!" He then said he was just joking. Boy if only he knew what my mind was thinking and my mouth wanted to say. If his ass wasn't a murderer, I would have fell prey to giving him the best ass whooping a bitch could find. But nope, not with this crazy, off-the-meds, cross-eyed, son-of-a-bitch! As I sat in the passenger seat, with my head leaned against the window I looked up towards the sky silently asking GOD "Why?" All to see yet another fucking full moon. Full moons bring out the craziness in folks. It was a full moon when I met him and now a full moon when his ass wants to act like lunchmeat. Ole stale bastard. This has pissed me off royally and I don't have no one to blame but myself. I got a certain type of person I like. Yeah right, I know the next god-dam time. Payback for not waiting on GOD. The thoughts overtook reality, but I couldn't express verbally what I truly needed to say. You right this shit ain't got nothing to do with the Lord, girl. You can't blame this one on HIM at all! See what happens when we don't wait on GOD. We get ourselves in some shit that we can't get out of and then we look to him for guidance and saving. Ain't no telling when HE going to rescue me from this mess. HE gone make me sit in it all because I chose to do things my way. Nobody got your back when you knee deep in shit. That's the game of life. You must win all by yourself. You even go to jail by yourself, just like this penitentiary motherfucker sitting in the driver's seat of my damn car. Handcuffs are designed for single use occupancy. I so wanted to yell and tell him to "GETCHO FUNKY ASS outta my car, you lying nigga!" but nope, this fool done tried to kill somebody. So that thought quickly got out of my head. If only I could have a button that I could push to throw his monkey-ass clean out the driver's seat into the fucking street. I would push that motherfucker so fast, he wouldn't know what hit his ass. That way we both would be rolling in different directions. But NOPE! Heffa going along for the ride on this one because that inner voice will get you killed by schizo-bi-polar motherfucker in the driver's seat of my damn car! Have you ever feared your life being in the hands of a stranger or someone you had love for? What was your initial reaction? What did you feel you could do to save yourself from harm? What was your intuition telling you to do? Did you have enough strength to follow your intuition?

He decided to run in and grab some things while I sat in the car. I know this was my time to crank up and speed off. But what if he came to my house and found me. I didn't want to do nothing stupid for fear of him retaliating against me. Yes, as you can imagine, there is a fear inside of me that says I need to stay calm and play this out. Upon return to the house, I didn't even want to get in the bed and close my eyes to go to sleep. I had him put on a comedy movie to keep me laughing and not doze off with something boring playing. He came downstairs and asked me to take the medicine he bought. After learning all that I did, I didn't hesitate to do anything out of the ordinary. Besides it was just cough syrup and the bottle had yet to be opened, so I did all he asked within reason. He said he got quite a few things for my cold and he even bought a pregnancy test. I looked at this monkey motherfucker and as I started to yell, another thought came to my mind. Bitch you better not! Bite your tongue and speak softly. I forgot who I was trying to yell at? I can't get this nigga mad. I had been in enough bad relationships in my life that cost me in the end so I asked him, "Why do you insist that someone is pregnant by you?" "What is it with you and a baby?" "I told you I have my tubes tied and haven't been pregnant in over 10 years since my son was born. I don't know what more I can tell you!" He replied that he was just ruling things out and wouldn't it be funny if I was. He said having my tubes tied don't mean shit. I took the medicine but I wasn't feeding into his antics. As the morning came, I got up quietly and went home. He had fallen off to sleep. I was relieved to get in my car and drive off. Once I got around the corner from out of his housing development, I breathed a sigh of relief. I drove as fast as I could home, changed clothes, and went to work. I had so much to get caught up on from being out for over a week. I hardly ever call out from work and it was hard for me to get back in the swing of things. He texted me around lunch time to check on me and wondered if I was going straight home from work or coming to his house. I replied and told him that I wanted to go home for the night. I was too tired. He never replied back afterwards. Instead, when I pulled up to my house, he was standing at my door waiting for me. He knew my times like clockwork. That was the scariest thing, because with him you never knew what he would be up to. Seeing him made me cringe because I didn't know what to expect. I now feared this man to death. He came in and ended up staying the night. This went on for about three long weeks. It was as if he was stalking me but I couldn't seem to get rid of him at all. Finally, he asked me to drop him off at home because he had to go see his probation officer the following morning. Thank GOD! He had been at my house for over three weeks and wouldn't leave, even when I went to work. He had been having his family bring him clothes as if he had moved in. When he asked me to drop him off at his house, he didn't take his clothes with him. I asked why, and he said when he comes back over he won't have to worry about bringing anything because it will already be there. WAIT! When you coming back over? What the hell is this fool doing? I don't want him nowhere near me, let alone in my home. He has clearly forced himself on me and my children's lives. Invaded my privacy. Invaded my home. I had become so miserable and depressed but how could I get him out or even get myself away from him. I was living a nightmare and no one to save me from my own mess. I had become so stressed these past three weeks that I noticed I had missed my cycle, my hair started coming out, and I was looking horrible in the face. I wasn't motivated to do anything not even go to work. I just wasn't happy anymore with who I was as a person. After I dropped him off at home, I went back home instead of going to work. I was drained and wanted to get some sleep in my own bed. For weeks while he was there, I slept on the couch while he laid upstairs. I would purposefully go downstairs to watch TV and fall sleep there with intentions. I had my rescheduled doctor's appointment that evening after I dropped him off. My doctor wanted to check my labs and levels. She said I didn't look good and appeared to be severely dehydrated. She advised me to go to the emergency room and get some fluids through IV. Instead, I asked her to give me antibiotics and let me rest for a few days before I decided to go that route for treatment. I didn't want to tell her of my living situation. I wanted more than anything to protect my home. As I was driving home, he called me and said he was going to stay at his house and that I should go home and get some rest. I still insisted that he get his clothes and he became upset as to why I felt the need to get his things out of my house. I immediately diffused the situation and calmly got off the phone. Mysteriously we didn't talk for the next couple of days. He didn't even call to check on me. I was relieved to have some space, but the scary part to this was that I didn't know what all he was up to. Quite frankly, I didn't care. Just as long as it wasn't with me.

The next morning, my doctor's office called and she wanted me to come to the office to discuss my test results. I refused to call and tell him any of this. I just wanted to discuss things with my doctor on my own. While I sat in the doctor's office waiting to be called back, he called to see where I was. Oh boy, here we go with the bullshit again. I informed him where I was and he became irate that I didn't ask him to go with me or even call him. That conversation turned into an argument that I wasn't ready for or even prepared to deal with. As my doctor walked in the room, I hung up the phone. She began by going over my labs and asked me how was I feeling and what was going on in my life. After I confided in her, she informed me that I was pregnant. I continued to talk as if I didn't hear her. Hoping I didn't hear her. Wondering what the fuck did she just say!!! As I collectively gathered my thoughts, I began to ask so many questions and so did she. Wondering how on earth I could be pregnant but then she began to explain the medical side of things knowing that I got my tubes tied years ago. The last thing on earth that I wanted was to be pregnant by this crazy fool. My doctor said it was highly likely that it's in my tubes and had to be removed immediately. That was a sigh of relief for me. There is no way I would ever think about having anybody's baby. I was done having children and wouldn't entertain the thought by no man who wanted them. Now I got to tell this fool and I am still in shock but knowing that the situation had to be diffused is what relieved me. On the way home, I stopped at the local pharmacy and bought seven pregnancy tests. Once I got home, I pissed on all of them. Hoping one would be negative. But nope. All of them motherfuckers said positive. How in the world did this happen? Here GOD go punishing me again.

I took the moment to call him, out of respect. He asked me to come over and talk to him. Although I was very hesitant, I just wanted this nightmare to be over. Once I arrived, he greeted me at the door. He had a big smile on his face and by this time, he had informed his family of the news. Everyone was excited except for me. He didn't tell them that it may be in my tubes. All they knew was that I was pregnant and it was as if I had given them the best thing since sliced bread. The more he kept touching my stomach, the sicker I got. I asked him to go downstairs with me so we could talk. As we sat on the bed, he kept wiping his nose. I offered him some tissue and he declined. I began to explain to him how I felt about the relationship and the baby. The more I told him that I didn't want this child and there is no way we could have this child, the angrier he got. He felt as if I was lying to him. The more I informed him that I wasn't lying, he wouldn't believe me. The conversation turned to a full blown argument. I had gotten up to try to leave because I didn't want a face to face argument with him. He grabbed my arm and spun me around to continue to talk to him face to face. I spun around and tripped over his boots falling hard to the floor. He didn't seem to care. In fact, he didn't even offer to pick me up. In fact, all he wanted was to get his point across. His rage was severe and I heard that anger all over again. He was someone I didn't even know. He kept expressing how I didn't take him serious and I was taking him for a joke. I clearly had no idea what he was talking about. While I lay on the floor from the fall, he jumped on top of me and sat on my stomach while holding my arms to the floor above my head. Yelling angrily about how his feelings didn't matter and I was like all the others. I yelled for help and cried for him to get off my stomach but he wouldn't get up. His strength was a lot stronger than mines and he had me pinned down to where I couldn't move. No one would come downstairs because they had turned on the music upstairs and closed the basement door. So it was just us. I was at the hands of this person I clearly hadn't known. I cried and cried for him to get off of me and that he was hurting me. When he realized that he was on my stomach, he jumped up and started yelling at me. Telling me to look at what I made him do. It was as if he blanked out and didn't realize what he was doing because of the anger. I managed to crawl up on the bed and noticed that I was moist in my underpants. I asked him to look to see if there was blood, and sure enough it was. He hurried and took me to the emergency room and when they did the ultrasound, there was only an empty hole and no child. He wept profusely. He didn't realize that this child was in my tubes and I asked the nurse not to say anymore. I was just glad that it was gone and this nightmare was going to be over. They kept me overnight after doing the procedure as 24 hour protocol. I insisted that he go home for the night so that I can rest and be left alone. Nothing could have prepared me for what I just went through. What in the world is going on? Who is this person? I immediately called my friend and finally had a chance to vent to her about what I have been dealing with. She expressed how sorry she was but also stated that she didn't want to get in the middle of anything. How can you get in the middle of things when your friendship should have been to ensure my safety? Why did you let me walk into the unknown? She informed me of his past and said she thought that he was cured from his issues. I asked her what sort of issues he had. She said that he was on drugs years ago and snorted cocaine. That explained why he kept picking with his nose and sniffing. She said yes, if he is doing that then he is still using drugs. The cocaine will leave a residue in the nose. OMG! What did I get myself into? She also told me that he had been in an out of jail for more than just the latest charges and he has a wrap-sheet but she wasn't sure all of what the other charges were. She went into little detail about the medication for schizophrenia and they found out that he hadn't been taking the medication which keeps him calm. She said it was something they started giving him while he was locked up but he was not like that when he went in. When he came home, he was a completely different person. I couldn't fathom everything she was telling me at that time. My mind was completely blown. I felt so betrayed by my so called friend that I hung up on her. I had nothing left to say. All I wanted to do was move away and never to be found by this character.

I was discharged the next day and took 24 hours to recoup and get rest. I informed his family that I was dropping his clothes off before I went to work. I was done! I didn't want nothing else to do with him. I bagged up everything he had in my house and took them to his. His niece said they hadn't seen him in a few days and she didn't know where he was. After all that I just found out, I feared the worse. He could be lurking around somewhere trying to find me. Who knows? I then proceeded to go to work the next day. His family kept calling me asking me had I talked to him in a joking kind of way. The day was strange and strange as hell. The kids decided they wanted to come home from their grand-parent's house after school. So I took the day, while I had use of a computer at work and began planning my options. I started looking for another house to move into. I had a good enough savings to pay for at least three months of rent upfront and all I knew was that I needed to move right away and fast. I found a few homes while searching on Craigslist and one of them responded right away with an immediate move-in. I scheduled a viewing that very day and was relieved to see that my plan was happening the way I wanted it to. I wasn't worried or afraid. When my mind is set to something, I will get it done! Determined and focus driven is how I have always been. After viewing the home, I called my brother-in-law to see if he was available with his truck to help us move in should I get accepted for the home. His truck was big enough to fit the entire house in at one time and that is what I needed. Something that would only be one trip and over. The landlord called me within two days after I sent him the documents he needed and asked if I could meet him at the home to sign the lease and pay for two months up front. I couldn't have been happier to finally be getting away from this hard chapter in my life and moving on. It brought tears to my eyes. I knew that I would have to talk to the kids and inform of what I was doing. I hadn't talked to them about this relationship because I didn't want them to have to worry or be afraid. They had been through enough over the years. I maintained my silence but reassured them that we would always be ok. I strategically planned how I was going to go about this move. I literally had one hour to get the house moved with one trip. That would require all hands on deck and all hands I could find to help me.

The next day he called me out of the blue. I didn't ask where he had been, why I hadn't heard from him, because at this point, I clearly didn't give a dam. He said he finally got home and needed to go cool off. He apologized for what he did to me and wanted to talk and make things work between us. He expressed how he needed me and that I was the best thing for him. This shit went in one ear and out the other but I continued with my quest to keep him calm. He said that he had an appointment to see his probation officer in two days and wanted to come over after that to discuss the relationship. He kept saying it was the only way we would be happy. Those words rang loudly in my ear. So I asked him what he meant by that comment. He would only say that he had to see me and he could explain but I was adamant on staying away from him and keeping things as calm as possible until I could move without being seen. No one or nothing was going to deter me from accomplishing my goal and getting as far away from him and this mess as quickly as possible. My fear turned to urgency at this point. I said I wasn't ready to talk and told him I needed more time. He said ok.

While I was at work, his niece called me and asked me if I had talked to him. Again, I didn't understand why everyone was calling me asking me the same damn question. What was really going on? I replied, "Yes, just a little while ago." We had small talk and then the kids called me on my other line. My son was angry because he said they came home and the house was broken into, that there was glass all over the kitchen floor, and the TVs were gone. The entire back sliding door glass was shattered. WHAT! Not my house! I was infuriated. Could this be why everyone is calling me at work trying to strike up these dumb conversations, pretending and acting as if they didn't know anything? The neighborhood was quiet. Low crime. My neighbors were retired folks. Good people. Who could do this in broad daylight? I didn't have company over or let folks know where I lived. He was the first person I let in my home. I didn't even allow the kids to have company and they had their friends over where their grandparents lived. I immediately informed my boss that I had to leave. My gut instinct told me he had something to do with it. Maybe he retaliated against me for not taking him back. Or maybe this was just who he was as a person? I was such a fool for this and this was my payback. I informed the kids to not touch anything. That I would be there shortly. I called the police to report the crime and they met me at the house. Upon arrival, the kids was standing outside on the front porch. My son said there was glass everywhere and the police advised me to stay outside while they went in to access the damages. They found a brick on the floor and suggested that it didn't look random but someone who I knew because of the way the entry happened and what was taken. The house wasn't ram-shacked or torn apart. The items were specific. The burglar targeted only what he or she knew would bring them money. All I could do was pray to my GOD to relieve me from this nightmare. This hellish nightmare. Why GOD? Why me? As distraught as I was, I was angrier at the fact that this was done to me. I don't bother no one. Absolutely no one!! After the police left, I called my brother-in-law. I had to put my plan in motion quicker than expected. I had to act fast and not waste any more time. I called the new landlord and immediately met with him, signed the lease, and got my keys to the new home. The house was advertised as ready to move in. My brother questioned the urgency to move and I had no choice but to be honest with him. He understood and suggested we center the move on the time he had to go see his probation officer. Again, remaining calm was hard but I had to assure him that nothing was wrong and we was good with our relationship. Later that evening, he called me and asked what time could he come over to talk with me. I gave small talk about his meeting with the probation officer and stated to him that he could come over when he was through. He was happy that I agreed to have him come see me. I also discussed with him about the break-in at my house. His reaction was somber and quiet with not much to say. I put the blame on someone random that the kid's may have known and stated that I scolded my son about bringing company home when I'm not there. This way I could throw him off and he wouldn't think I suspected it was him. I didn't pack up a thing. He said he had to meet his officer at 1:00 p.m. Perfect timing! That gave me time to get everything out of the house no later than 2:00 p.m. Those meetings usually last about an hour he said. I informed the kids that they are not going to school and I won't be going to work because we will be moving. They seemed relieved and happy. The next morning I called him right before he left his house to go to his meeting. He had a ride and they was getting in the car to leave. After we talked, I called my brother to come to the house and move everything out at once. With the kids help, we loaded the truck up in 47 minutes. My townhouse was small but we got it done. He called me to let me know he was on his way to my house. I didn't let him know anything different was going on. I just replied, "Ok" all the while, the last load was being loaded on the truck and we was getting ready to pull off. We were finally free from everything. A sigh of relief. I didn't look back or go back to see if I left anything valuable. I didn't care anymore because material things are replaceable, but my life was not. Immediately after I hung up from him, I called the phone company to change my number. This was the only way I could handle the situation and I had no regrets. I couldn't have any regrets. I needed to be free. I asked them to give me a few hours to retrieve my messages and clear my phone out. As I listened to my messages, he had called me with death threats because the house was empty when he got there. He was ranting about how he would find me and do harm to me. After retrieving my messages, I had the number changed. I resigned from my job and began searching for another. My co-workers called me and informed me that he had been calling and came up there. This was the only way and I felt like the last incident was the beginning to no end. It was just getting started with him. My kids and I have suffered enough at the hands of mental and physical abusive people. This had to end this way. His demons continued to chase him until one day they caught up with him. He lost his life at the hands of another man's gun several months' later. KARMA!

Huit: Green Grass!

You know we always think that the grass is greener on the other side until we get to the other side. The misconception that someone will treat me better than the last is at times wishful thinking to say the least. What if what we had in the beginning was good treatment but through foolish eyes, we thought it was bad. What role do you feel you played to create the bad situation? Did we speak of change to make it better? Did we live through the mouths of fools and babes while refusing to follow the matters of our own heart?

Instead we decided to find flaws of which we couldn't or didn't want to get past or even get over. We forced our minds to accept things like:

- He isn't good enough

- He is not my type
- He drinks too much
- He wasn't head-strong enough for me
- He was lazy in bed
- He not a clean person
- He not financially stable
- He acts ghetto
- He not smart enough
- He was selfish
- He doesn't complete me

Outward appearances that retracted the mind to reject the matters of the heart are just that. They are things we see and judge before getting to know the inside man. Are these changeable things or are they willing to change within themselves to make us reconsider why we chose them in the 1st place? Without thought, we took the easy road. We searched for what we thought was better. We searched for what we thought would complete our ideal package of what we view as today's complete man. These standards that was set forth by mommy and daddy at a younger age. The standards that gave us the polish look on the outside and covered the blemishes on the inside. To us who seek in the end, that's all that mattered, right? The polished look! But do they matter at all? You constantly hear the opinionated words of outsiders making the decisions that became easy to you. So there you have it! Everyone on the outside will always be in agreeance with the choices you make through foggy lenses viewed through daily. But we must remember, they are on the outside looking in through your foggy lenses. So if the vision is not all that clear, what are you truly seeing? Who does this person appear to be to you? When you finally gave in to the foolery, you channeled your heart to say that GOD will reveal what you need to see, IF there is anything to see. We dare not go searching and not have our hearts prepared for what we may find. So now we put this on GOD because we refused to see the truth but we settle for the blemishes. Blemishes that aren't clear. Blemishes are foggy abstracts for what we hope is truth. What we hope is real! GOD reveals all things good, bad, or indifferent through clear lenses. When the revelations were shown, we choose NOT to wipe the lenses clean before viewing.

I settled! Settling was easy sometimes. I became complacent. Be it with work, relationships, and my all- around daily habits become routine when I truly needed a change. I settled for the dam good, bad, and indifferent. Boy, what a combination of foolery I chose to now deal with. That tall glass of water will choke the shit out of you in the end! Mark my word! I went to the other side walking in my own faded glory because I had had enough. I wanted a change in my life and it seems I got what I asked for. I had known of him for 15 years, a blast from my past. All I ever wanted was to finally be called his lady and not have to ever feel hurt or pain again or so I thought! Love is painful, just like beauty but they all come with a price to pay. I put the past behind me and instead of forgiving the past, I chose to ignore it and move forward blindly. I wanted to put it behind me and start this walk fresh. I was always told to leave the past in the past. Should I live in the past then I will never move forward. That's what I was taught and I did just that! The first month was going well. No complaints. No problems. No worries. Long term plans was made with promises from both of us. We finally got back together again after 15 years of complete separation. Throughout those years we had run-ins with each other, however, we never reconnected in such a way that would allow us to commit to a relationship but only a friendship, as he wanted us to be labeled. Just friends! Our feelings grew more and more with each passing day until THAT day when a red flag was thrown in the game. The term back in the day was a "monkey wrench." A flag that reminded me of the past, sent my mind racing, looking, wondering! The more I questioned the flag, the more the other became aggravated. He repeatedly told me that my mouth was going to give us a lot of problems with moving forward. He wasn't used to a woman being vocal, he said. Ok. So let me digress this bullshit. In other words, he wanted a woman to only do as he said and not have an opinion. Oh I forgot that my Freedom of Speech was just taken from me. OK…So now I couldn't question the validity of the facts found because the other viewed that as their past and didn't want to live there. For a minute there, I forgot the year I was living in. WOW. Well I be damned. Really. Ok. So I let it rest and continued to move forward, right! They said time heals all wounds. But not if the motherfuckers keep popping the hell up! Right! Another week went by and there were several more monkey wrenches thrown in the game that needed my undivided attention. Instead of voicing, I kept quiet and observed with my analytical ass. This shit got me pulling out my investigative hat, sneaking and snooping trying to catch a case. You would think folks would grow up and get tired of game playing. They say silence is golden but in this case, there was this black cloud over a sunny day! Hell it was raining every day around this foolishness. I tried channeling my good energy into positive behaviors, but I couldn't get past the monkey wrenches. The more I thought about them, the more things didn't feel right within my spirit. I prayed and prayed for things not to be true. I asked GOD to reveal to me accurate information, but I wasn't prepared mentally for what I was asking for. I wanted to be wrong! I was patient because HE works in his own timing. Until it is revealed, I must endure. I know my GOD and I know it will be just a matter of time before things are revealed. I refused to entertain the past by accepting the day to day foolery that was put before me. After a week of basking in the foolery, it was revealed to me through clear lenses this time. You see back in the day when we met and I caught him in a lie, he would always turn his mouth up and look down on you. So that let me know he was lying. Well here we are 15 years later and I asked him a series of questions and he gave me the same dam gesture. Now I gotcho ass… you lying monkey. So what did I do, I started twitching my dam mouth up and looking up at him all the same. The only difference was, the monkey in the room was doing the lying and I had him by the balls. He didn't even realize I was already ten steps ahead of him with the game. This big leopard never changed his spots. We was two mouth twitching motherfuckers, it's just that he was the one doing the lying and I was going to enforce the punishment. See, I considered myself a fair player of the game. In the beginning of any friendship or relationship:

I'ma tell yo azz I'ma find out so don't try!
I'ma tell yo azz to be honest, so don't lie!
I'ma tell yo azz…
I'ma tell yo monkey motherfucking azz!
ONE GOD-DAM TIME

But guess what? You did what the hell I told you not to do. So that means you get what you don't think you're going to get! Now it was time for me to put myself into action. "Protection of the heart" is my rule of thumb. I started calling him from my stakeout points. I wasn't angry, hurt, sad, or furious with such rage that reacting would put me in a bad situation to lose and I couldn't afford that. I called and called and the other would never pick up the phone to speak as I sat in my car there through my clear lenses. I had my car positioned so well, that I had a clear, clean view to his front door. I can see you but you dam sure as hell couldn't see me! So, I texted him and let him know I was dropping by…. Uh-oh the pop-up game! You know you wrong for that shit. Any other time I can call and pop up but not this day…. Oh really… My way of thinking was if you allow me the opportunity to knock once…. God-Dammit I'm knocking all the dam time until you say stop…. And I haven't heard you say stop yet! KNOCK KNOCK Fool! Less than five minutes went by and no reply to my text message. But something told me not to move and don't send another message to him. GOD said "peace be still." So I sat patiently. Watching. A sense of calm came over me this day. Actually, I had a smile on my face and I began to chuckle inside. Almost as if victory was won. But the show wasn't even over yet. Or was it over before it even began? So as I watched from my location, something said don't move…keep your eyes focused…. 5...4...3...2...1. The front door opens and both of them monkeys come rushing out. One in front of the other. She is being rushed off to her car, while he stands there with little conversation. Tank-top t-shirt, shorts, and a pair of flip flops is what he wore for the special movie premier called… "Get Your Ass Outta My house Heffa!" I shocked myself and wasn't even mad. I actually started to laugh because I wanted to see what was going to happen next. Hell had I texted: "It's a bomb in the motherfucking house," I betcha that monkey would have ran out with boxes of his most prized possessions: expensive watch collection, TVs, slippery earls, a host of his most braggable, sliceable items he can't stop talking about within conversation. For him, relationships were a Soap Opera and he was the Leading Man casted for the part. This fool slipping and sliding through relationships wearing cheap ass shoes while keeping track of time wearing cheap ass watches from the pawn shop. Oh, did I forget the cologne that smelled like hot ass on a 98 degree day, sweating between the cheeks. Just the thought of it makes me role my dam eyes backwards and wish the MOST prized possession was larger than a 16 year old boy. He was a shover anyway. You all know what a shover is? A nigga who can't get up but wants to shove his shit in you in order to get a hard on. A fucking shover! That baby don't know all that medication will make you limp. Check your health first, fool! Hell I can't talk, that shit got me stalking the monkey. It's a known fact that once a cheater, always a cheater, I guess. About 3 minutes later after he returned to his living quarters, I received a text reply. Like really fool! My next act of kindness was to clarify the behavior of idiots with knowledge. The facts!! The foolery!! But guess what happened, HE DENIED IT! Don't you just hate when niggerdum takes precedence over the truth! You see things with your own eyes and deliver facts as they are and the other blatantly denies things. In fact, I got blamed! Blamed for being someone they thought I could never be. That's what the other said to me. It was MY fault. All mines. The other even had the nerve to say he was appalled that I would even insinuate these lies. Well I be damned! Now it's my fault for finding out the truth. REALLY! The only lie he could come up with was to blame me and run from the truth due to EXPOSURE! The lies and deceit of the other was throughout the 15 years but there is a difference between then and now. Not only are we much older but you would have thought immature behavior would have dismissed itself along with the mental issues the other was dealing with many years ago. It was 15 years ago when the other said they was dealing with mental issues and things. They finally shared this news in the beginning of our reconnection and that was their reason for their actions towards me at that time. Blame it on the brain! OK… But now that the brain has healed and cleansed itself to make you a righteous man of GOD, the games should receive a cease and dismiss order. You would think! I guess they missed getting served by the law of the mighty words of GOD because you are still playing the same old games, fool! 15 years later! This makes it even worse because now you are very well aware mentally of your actions and you performed them with bad intentions. How do I internally process that type of behavior? GOD doesn't lie to me, so why did you! Internally, I wanted to react. Internally, I wanted to confront you and whoop your natural monkey ass. Internally, the war is far from over! Vengeance is mine said the LORD. Internally, has now rested with karma and I can promise you it will come for you! The power of prayer can do wonders when least expected! We need to be mindful of HIS punishments when attacking GODs children with lies, deceit, and malice. The many tears I have shed in the past over the other was unimaginable. I spoke with my child, who I thought wouldn't have remembered the other. I was informed that they remember the sadness, the tears, and the loneliness from the lies told. The memories were not good memories but her words of encouragement softened the heartache not the blow.

The pain endured by love can create the most destructive atmosphere. The anger and rage is often times uncontrolled and it isn't until the aftermath is over, that we begin to see what damage was done. Should I care about the damage because at the end of the day, the heart was shattered unrepairable? We think the grass is greener on the other side because we made excuses not to love what GOD had already given us. Sometimes, seeking outside the yard can grow more weeds than flowers. I guess you can say, sometimes we like to play in the dirt! If we went out to cut the grass on a regular basis and tended to the yard, we can see that pretty flowers will begin to bloom year after year.

Gardening is hard work. You're pulling weeds, trimming hedges, cutting grass while dealing with insect vultures along the way. In hindsight, a relationship is built the same way. It takes work to create a beautiful flower that is stable enough to sustain on its own year after year. Granted, there will be fights, disagreements, laughs, tears, and smiles, but if we use patience and guidance with great communication, in time, it will be all worth it in the end! Jumping to fast before the work is done can cause destruction with GODs project. It is very important to love without expectation. If we are always expecting of others, we are setting ourselves up for mere disappointment when we don't receive a return. Love should come without a cost. The issue arise when the love given is under false pretenses. We all know what we can give and who we want to give in to immediately at that moment of interaction. Greed takes over because what is put on the table, we feel, isn't enough to keep the belly full. We eat and take without stopping to swallow for fear of never having enough to complete us. But what if it is and why do we feel we need more?

Communication is key in all types of relationships. Be it at work, grocery store, and even at home. If it's your child, parent, significant other, or boss, we all must effectively communicate to get understanding of each other. Running away solves nothing! Facing our situations head on without fear of losing is the best option. If we should loose, it won't be the first nor the last. The world won't come to an end! The only thing that it says is it wasn't meant to be. LIFE as we know it and live it, comes with all types of situations. Either we learn from them and grow with the next obstacle, or we continue to be complacent with our stumping growth.

I empower you to plant the seed, pull the weeds, trim the hedges, and cut the grass in your own yard. Watch the flowers bloom slowly but surely. It will take some time and there is no need to rush. Things will start out rocky, but with some nurturing and communication, things will begin to stabilize with normalcy. We must ensure that patience is at the forefront of all we do, because Rome wasn't built in a day neither was the growth of life. Relationships operate in the same manner. We put up walls of defense to protect and shield our hearts from harm because no one wants to feel hurt or pain. It may take some caressing and soft spoken words in order for the other to begin to bring down the guards slowly. In the end it is all worth it with a MIGHTY lesson to learn!

But you, Daniel, shut up the words and seal the book, until the time of the end. Many shall run to and fro, and knowledge shall increase." *Luke 21:36ESV*

Neuf: Carolyn's Song

"Ang, Shanta, Bonita wake up." Momma said. As momma gathered us up and got us dressed for the sitters, she said, " I got some errands to run and I gotta take yall next door for a little while." Nothing prepared us as children for what would happen next or become of us. Momma hurried us to the next building and dropped us off at the neighbors. She gave kisses on the forehead and informed the neighbors that she would be back in the afternoon. Because momma was in a hurry and I assumed she was going to work or had even gotten a new job. She was young, just 21 years of age and already had three small children ages three, five, and six. She came to Maryland from North Carolina searching, chasing, and all alone. Thought that things would get better while here but where she came from was a lot better than where she landed. Mom and Dad got divorced after I was born, 1972 but still continued to see each other. Dad had come to the north at the age of 17 searching for a better life with work and left Mom in the south, but Mom couldn't wait, she had to come up North on her own. She couldn't sit still long enough to allow patience to be her virtue. She got an apartment in the city of Landover, Maryland where she took up residence. As momma dropped us off, she gave us all a kiss on the cheek and scurried about her way. The neighbors were white, middle aged couple who had no children of their own. The day grew long and it started to get dark outside. We all was wondering when was momma coming back. Even the neighbors. I remember sitting at their dinner table that night, eating what smelled of burnt rice with the memory of what else was on my plate appeared vague in my memory. To this day, I don't eat white rice and should I ever, it will have to have a gravy or broth cooked in it because plain white rice still and will always have a stench of burnt smell to it reminding me of that day. It was the following morning and momma didn't appear to come get us like she said she would. We all began to cry and I remember the couple talking about whether or not they should call the police or wait. The man stated "No, let's wait and see if the mom or dad will appear. A few days went by and there was a knock on the door. Momma and Daddy Appeared in the doorway and the encounter wasn't good for momma. Who would have thought that would be the last time I would see my momma? We spent many years after that being raised in Rocky Mount, North Carolina. Raised by my dad's mother, aunts, and uncles. Soon daddy came for us and needed us near him here in Maryland. With an empty heart of not knowing and needing my mother figure, I endured a lot as a child. All I knew was that Maryland was the last place I saw momma and I needed to find her and see her. Almost 8 years went by and no sign of momma. No other woman in my dad's life filled the whole in my heart. That piece was for my momma and I was that determined child to find her.

With parenting, I was a child who wanted understanding from all sides. I was told there are always three sides to the truth: Moms, Dads and the Lords. Through trajectory, we remember occurrences, times, faces, feelings, and without closure, we are left wounded. Being wounded and unhealed will make us open and subjective to constant conflict and confrontations, carried anger and aggression taken out on those not warranted.

Being able to identify those internal issues are sometimes forgotten with time and more-so lack of self-growth internally. As we age, we tend to go back to the beginning of things while trying to combat acts of aggression, pain, unresolved emotions, and rage. All those feelings that are outside the scope of normal behaviors. We would also refuse to tap into those emotional feelings because of fear. Fear of what we might do or say. Fear of the unknown will make us want to forget and continue this walk with our unhealed souls. So what do you think you would do should you ever want to heal your heart and soul? How would you begin? Where would you start?

I was just 15 years old when I wanted to find my Momma. You see, the last time I saw Momma, I was six years of age and things didn't go according to her parenting plan. She left us and I was empty, angry, and not withstanding to open up to another woman who felt she wanted to give me motherly love. I was that child who acted out with rebellion and no matter what, I wasn't going to replace my mother with another. It just wasn't going to happen. I am forever grateful for those that stepped in and very appreciative however, what's in my heart is clearly where my heart will lead me. There is always one child out of the bunch who may never forget and I guess I was the chosen one. No matter what the age when trajectory happens in your life, you tend to remember something about that incident no matter how big or small. I was the one who always paid the most attention to everything and who didn't allow you to forget nothing. I know some of you have experienced that with a child who reminded you of what you said and didn't do. Some will even go a step further and tell you what you need to do and won't do. These are "new millennium" children as I call them.

By the time I found momma, she had two more children. I had two brothers named Lamont (Bunt) and Foday Mohammed (Deenie). Lamont had a smile that would light up a room. He had a gentle and loving spirit that was so infectious. Deenie, loved to laugh. Bowlegged and could outrun a cheetah. They both loved playing football with their Uncle Stevie and Uncle Michael every day after school. Happy kids was an understatement to say the least. They both was even more fascinated when they found out they had sisters. They carried that love daily with them through their walk on this earth. They didn't bother you unless you bothered them or those they loved the most, which explained why they were the keepers of their own sheep. You would have thought they came from the wound at the same time. They were inseparable. They were my heartbeats and meant the world to me. I didn't want to spend a day without them. Although only a few years apart in age, they were inseparable. There was not a day that went by where I didn't want nothing more than to be with my momma and my brothers. They were my heartbeats. I had just had my first child of which I had to give up for adoption and although they took some of the pain away, the void will forever be remained until. I meet my child again in this world. My momma wasn't told of that child, but I know if she had been, my son would still be with me. Momma would surely have taken him and raised him for me. She was heartbroken by what I had to share with her, knowing that she has a grand-child out here in this world she would never get to know but she showed me what unconditional love truly was. The simple things like a kiss on the cheek, or telling me she loved me without expectation, was all my heart needed to survive. I hadn't heard much of those things or received those things growing up. It was all too purposeful when I received them from my momma. She taught me how to give love in return without expectation from any. She purified my heart in such a way that I could survive off the bare minimum of life without realizing that I needed more than what was given because my heart stayed full continuously. I was raised hard through the lessons I was given, and she showed me the soft side to life which gave me the balance I needed to grow with my own. My mother's love was pure, wholesome, and balanced. It completed me and fulfilled my heart to beat a little longer inside its caved walls of shelter. It was love at its purist form. Created by the most virtuous woman living in a simple, perplexed bubble. Untouchable. Angelic. Purified.

Carolyn suffered more than the eyes could see. She wrote in faith and love without asking for anything in return. Writing was her music to its own built lyrics that had award winning verses never skipping a beat. She was humorous and loved to crack jokes. When she saw you down or sad, she would create funny nicknames that would make you laugh. Names that would make you forget why you was ever mad or sad. Life to her was just that! Life. A strong yet simple four letter word with a big meaning. She never complained nor did she regret how her destination was mapped out. She would always say, "It's in GODs hands, baby. We gotta do what HE say and find a way!" Momma never made excuses or waivered from truths! When I found momma, I didn't care about why she left us on the doorsteps of a white family. She fed my soul with what I needed and had yearned for all my life. I needed the kiss on the cheek, I needed the hugs and sentimental words that everything will be ok. I needed not to be blamed for things I didn't do. But not for one second did she spare the discipline. She just had a way of doing it so it wouldn't hurt the heart so bad. She filled my heart with a Mother's love and only a child's recipient would know what that felt like, especially when it came from your biological mother. As an adult, we tend to miss or forget the innocence of those childlike things. The bosom of where you lay nested to grow and flourish. An instantaneous moment of reconnection. A match made in heaven and only GOD knew how to reconnect Adams Rib with Eves Loins. That's the real, true, yet ideal connection between mother and child. It was at that point, I forgave my mother for all that she did and didn't do for me. GOD allowed us many chances at life to get it right and start over. HE connected the ribs and made us whole. From that day forward, we vowed to never lose contact no matter where this earth landed us. I ensured that my mother would never walk this earth without the feeling of a child's love bestowed upon her heart and she ensured that I graced this earth knowing what a mother's love felt like in return.

All in its simplest forms!

I knew my mom had reservations about things. The reconnection from the start seemed too good to be true. Although she had two other children, the loss of her daughters left a void in her heart and her life. I later found that my brothers never had the love of their fathers. So in essence we all had voids that needed to be filled. My mother gave all the love her breath could withstand. She gave her all and made the best of every opportunity given, even her second chances. There were a lot of questions that circled my brain but my mom reassured me that she would do her best to answer them with the upmost of truth. She didn't shy away from nothing and took full responsibility for her actions and roles she played in the outcomes of all situations. That is what I loved the most about her. She would always say to me, “Shanta, mankind can’t stand to be told the truth about themselves, but no matter what, don’t you ever shy away from it. Lying gets you nowhere!” That is the creed I live by and carry my torch doing daily. Being honest and sticking to my truths is the only way to live this earth. Honestly, she was right. Folks can’t stand the truth no matter how much it hurts them. I got so cocky with it growing up that I began telling folks the truth and didn’t give a damn about how they felt afterwards. Now, I tell the truth with compassion. Whatever that means. My mom told me that sometimes she felt like she was talking to my dad. Rough with words. So she taught me to be more compassionate but still get my point across. She reversed a lot of wrongs in my life as a young woman that I needed. We all need balance but we must also be mindful of who we receive that balance from. Mines was my momma. I knew and identified my emptiness. I knew and identified my anger. I knew and identified my void. I knew what I was missing most in my life. I couldn’t walk this earth without finding that piece of me that I knew I needed most: HER

The day I laid eyes on her, was the day GOD took the weight of the world off of my shoulders. The day my mother saw me and hugged me, she said, "Baby, I knew you would find me. I knew you wouldn't let me down. I thank you for loving me still in your heart. I'm so so so sorry!" THAT was all I needed to hear! Life was as simple as that for me. That was the first hug I received from my mom since I was 6 years old and it felt soooo damn good to my soul.

Have you ever found what your heart desired most? The absence of a person healed you in such a way that no one else in this world mattered. There was no other existence but the two of you at that moment. All you wanted to do was feel their skin, smell them, touch them and never let them go. Was it is at that time when you felt like nothing could harm or hurt you? You was safe in their rapture. The emptiness existed no more. The past was left in the past. Completely forgotten for that moment. Blistful. You felt free and no matter what happened in the past, you was no longer held in bondage because of it. As I stood with my eyes closed, and embraced my momma, the world existed no more except with she and I.

We had a beautiful relationship as well as a friendship. I had my special time's with my mom celebrating Mother's day, Thanksgivings, Christmas, and just because days. I spent so much time with her that life was carefree with her by my side. No matter what we never lost contact with each other, ever. When my brothers got older, they came to live with me and helped me take care of my children. The kids loved every bit of it. They had the best times of their life. It was just us. They were the centerpiece of our world until the ways of the world took them from us. The clouds turned grey for us on the morning of April 4, 2004. My momma was getting up early for the day. It was the special day for her because it was her birthday and the weekend was here. She stood in the living room of her 2 bedroom apartment early this morning. She was singing and prancing because GOD allowed her to see another year of her life. "POW! POW! POW! POW! POW! POW! POW!" She quickly ran to her balcony door and heard what sounded like gunshots just steps away from the building door. She saw commotion but didn't think nothing of it and proceeded to go back in the house to get clothes on. Suddenly, neighbors began yelling her name, "Ann!" "Ann!" "It's Bunt, they shot Bunt!" She ran as quickly as she could out the building, all to see her son lying on the ground, face down riddled with bullet holes. It was at that moment she realized that the person shot was her son. He was chased by these guys and tried to make it to the building, home to his momma. A 9MM handgun and one shot to the chest was all it took. The shooters' fled after they saw my brother drop to the ground. My oldest brother, Lamont, was murdered by his so-called friends. Guys that my momma fed daily and especially on Sunday's for dinner. Guys that raved about my momma's homemade mac and cheese. Guys that thanked her daily for taking them in and giving them love that they hadn't ever received from their own. Shot seven times over a simple argument that required a handshake, but you killed her loving child all because you couldn't beat him with your own two hands. There is always some kind of jealousy amongst so called friends, but this kind took a life that meant so much to so many people. He wouldn't bother a soul but he would open up the can of whoop ass if, and only if, you messed with those that was near and dear to him. That is how this started. Over a fight the night before protecting his brother and he handled his business. Instead, you kill him like a coward because you couldn't hurt him any other way.

My mother suffered in silence but never complained about the internal.

She still had one son she had to look after in this world and it wasn't easy for her. She began receiving death threats towards him and we found it best for her to move back home to North Carolina. Those threats soon followed 8 months later, during the night of Christmas Eve, my baby brother came running down the street towards mommas house yelling, "Mommaaa! Mommaaa! Mommaaa!" It was at that moment when my uncles ran outside and saw my brother engulfed in flames. My uncles threw a sheet over him the put the flames out but it was too late. He was unrecognizable and burned over 100% of his body. He was set on fire yet his soul was still a live vessel yearning for our mother. I never forget getting that call from my momma on Christmas morning. The hurt in her voice, the emptiness in her heart. Her soul praying to GOD to take her life because she felt unworthy to live another day on the earth. GOD said, "No my child, you still have unfinished business to tend to." She couldn't stop crying long enough to get the words out to tell me what was going on. My children decided to celebrate Christmas on Christmas Eve in honor of my brother, their uncle, from that day forward. Christmas Day will forever be our day of remembrance for my brother "Deenie."

Carolyn never complained nor did she waver any hard feelings towards anyone. In fact, she wanted to go to the jail and speak to the young men who took her babies lives. She said "Baby, I don't understand why they didn't just come to me and talk to me before killing him like that. I fed those boys. I was like a mother to those boys! Their parents weren't around, so why did they hurt me like that." She still remained a mother to them in spite of the wicked things they did. She said all they needed was a hug and for her to tell them that she loved them in spite of what they did. Her heart may have been heavy but she still walked this earth praising God, singing to the beat of HIS music, and holding out for HIM to fulfill the void of emptiness in her heart. Because of her faithfulness to the community and its' children, the city of College Park wrote an article on her. My momma made the front page. She and I laughed about that months later and she told me to keep it and hold on to it. Through loss, she still smiled. Through loss, she rose again to see another beautiful day. The courage of this woman was amazing! She was a silent fighter! She said "that is what GOD is for: fighting!" She knew HE needed her to sit still while he battled life's transgressions and she obeyed like the most humble servant. My job was to continue giving the love and ensuring that my children gave her the love she needed. I vowed to never allow my mother to walk this earth not knowing and feeling the love of her child. I vowed to my mother to always know that she wasn't alone in this world. I vowed to my mother that I appreciated her for being her. The rawness of her. The realness of her. The naturalness of her in the most simplistic way. GOD fulfilled her heart again and allowed it to beat to its own drum when HE gave her Howard Coleman. That man loved his Carolyn and it was "Til Death Do Them Apart."

On April 05, 2014 my mother left me to go home to the LORD. It was the early morning hours around 6:00am, she tried to get up and take her blood pressure medicine and collapsed while having a heartache. I didn't receive all the calls because I turned my phone off that day. My daughter's birthday was the day. She went to a party and had consumed an illegal substance and life turned upside down. That was a saga within itself consumed me!
The loss of my mom left a big whole in my life, yet temporary. GOD showed my mom favor and made her heart whole by giving her a husband to spend the rest of

her life with. He loved her madly and it was their world to conquer. Momma gained patience and GOD rewarded her for her obedience. She and Howard danced to their own music. We had been talking the days prior and making arrangements for her to come up North with me. I had even gotten her apartment back at the senior building where she used to live some years ago. I was going to pick her up and bring her back up North but she insisted I stay here and complete my final exams. She always said to me "Don't let nothing or no one come in between your studies, not even me." She said she and Howard would make it back just fine and we started laughing about him being blind but could still see in the dark. She told me not to worry about nothing and that she would see me soon enough. She died the day after my daughter's birthday, April 5th. I wasn't given the opportunity to say my proper goodbyes to her which left me traumatized in the worse way, both mentally and physically. The devil had been busy that week and if it wasn't for my faith in GOD, I could have done unnecessary damage out of rage and anger. When things are out of your control no matter what is being told, lies take precedence over truth. I knew the most important thing in my mom's life was to always walk this earth with me. We vowed to never leave each other's side no matter what and I honored that. The day of her funeral, her remains had been signed over to me. I wasn't surprised but hurt that I couldn't see her, hug her, kiss her, touch her skin, hold her hand, or even caress her beautiful natural hair just one last time. All I wanted was one last time to see my momma, just one! I was denied that!! I was denied that!! After the funeral, everyone left going their separate way. I asked my aunt to take me and momma to the bus station to go home. I proudly strapped my mom's warm remains to my chest, hopped on the Megabus and came home. Momma, I held my head high just as you taught me to do no matter what. With me is where she will always be. My life, since losing my three amigos, most important people besides my very own children, has been pretty damn good. Momma has been my good luck charm! My mom was a writer but never got a chance to publish her story. I vowed to do so respectfully.

"Ok GOD, time to move on!"

I love you madly Carolyn Ann McMillan

Til death do us part!

Ten: Undivided Attention

My first apartment, I was given a large Print bible as a housewarming gift. My first Bible. I was informed that no matter what I went through in life, my daily walk was with the Lord's Prayer, Psalm 123 (all verses). My other favorite verse in all of the madness was Psalm 91:1. Emergency! I was told to place this Bible as the centerpiece on my table and to never allow it to move to different locations throughout the house. Since 1990, this Bible has been my rock as tattered and torn as it is and possibly tired of moving from place to place, but it has maintained its worth in my life. Traveled with me through all of my highs and lows.

Prayer

Faith of a Mustard Seed

Beliefs

Strength

Courage

Endurance

GOD's Children

As I walked through darkness, I found I was never alone. I had the love of GOD and my children to carry me through. While doors were closed in my face and backs were turned, I refused to allow "Shame" to take up residence in the home of where my heart lived. I accepted none of it. My children heard the screams and cries for help. They saw the bruises and witnessed the punches. They saw the scars and wondered if they would ever heal. Mommy promised them they would heal and so would we. Those words of promises are what has kept the fight in me alive. ANYTHING for my babies! I refused to hide from "SHAME!" I refused to push them aside as if they didn't matter or exist. I couldn't control the actions of others only mine. In the absence of their fathers, they completely belonged to me!

Who would take care of my children? Who would feed and clothe my babies? They were already fatherless, so I played dual roles without complaining. I didn't want them to ask the question of "How" or ‘Why” especially when I knew what all had to be done to accomplish the unknown. Things just had to get done by any means necessary. I had to ask myself time and time again if the fight was done in vein and not have a purpose. Try looking in your own babies eyes and answer their questions with assurance. I know your answer will be like mine and your fight with be just as vicious. The more they needed, the more I fought. The more I fought, the more GOD gave. It was as if I was fighting with life to sustain it and fighting with GOD not to take me with him. Each time HE left me alone. Stubborn fool one would say! But was the fight more with the Devil himself, and it was GOD who won the battle! Maybe. I was told that the battle was never mine but the LORDs. I started believing what the Christians told me blatantly to my face.

The daily reading and reciting of GODs words is what kept me. The belief in what he spoke and wrote is what humbled me. The art of his sacrifice is what saved me. There was no other love to give me and I wasn’t ready to die trying to search for another unjustified.

My Mom always told me to learn to write to GOD daily. He will read my heart led by the pen, should it be sincere. So each night I began to write out my fears, pains, and wishes. Ending with blessings. I wrote during turmoil and triumphs, while also writing with smiles. Each night before closing my eyes, I wrote out what occurred that day. Then getting on my knees to pray for the indifference through busted lips, swollen eyes, aching hearts, I prayed. Crying for an ending. Crying for peace. Crying for forgiveness. Crying to be saved! The more I cried and prayed for strength to endure all battles faced, the more HE gave me what I humbly asked for. I implore each of you to give second chances as your "Higher" power gave you time and time again. The reward of it has not only been a blessing but completed me as a human. We all need them. We all make mistakes intentional and unintentional. Forgive those and love in spite of. Make peace with matters of all hearts. Give all burdens to your spiritual father and allow HIM to carry the weight of the world on HIS shoulders, not yours! What we must remember is this: Every human purpose is intended to walk your path, but not intended to stay on it with you. Take from that walk, lessons to heal, learn, and teach from within.

After each tumultuous situation, I would say "OK, GOD, time to move on!" Then I moved on to another all to pick up where I left off prior. I would prevail and overcome all to repeat my dialogue to GOD again saying, "OK, GOD, time to move on!" Not realizing all HE wanted me to do was sit still and listen! WOW. The storm lasted 20 years. A lot of bumps and bruises, internal and external, not realizing that all HE wanted from me was my "Undivided Attention!"

About the Author

At the age of 52, GOD says now I Am Healed. All stories told are actual events in my life, yet HE has allowed me to see the reasons through the seasons. I have soared above the skies and conquered most in this world. I have 5 beautiful children who has not allowed me to give up on things important and learned from those less important. I currently work in the medical field of Nurse Administration with an abundance of certifications within my field. Adding "Author" to the list just ensures that my life lived has not been in vain, but it's purposeful with continuing to help others outside of my scope of practice. I am a fearless warrior with a heart of gold. Defining life's divine purpose should be everyone's fulfillment while the flesh exists on earth. I write with a purpose and that is to heal, but first I had to heal from within. I am and will forever be Carolyn's daughter!

<u>Scarred Tissue: Underneath It All</u>* is a biography of real-life events showcasing my true survival of relationship death and mental and physical abuse. It was my belief and faith in GOD that

gets tested time and time again. Although occurrences existed, I never wavered because of these tests given. I failed searching for love. I lost searching for love. I nearly died searching for love. I pushed forward raising her four children through shame and embarrassment, while walking in silence searching for her fifth child. If you have ever been faced with such trajectories in your life, not wondering what the outcomes would be, then you can clearly relate to the same situational acts of survival as the author has shared. Trajectories so profound that you never imagined that you would still be standing to tell your story. Yearning for your higher power to save you from the wrath while ensuring that your children will be ok through it all. My 1st book of a 3-part series depicts some of my stories of strength and courage to heal and become whole again while choosing to use my platform to help others in need for both men and women. The reasons why I am sharing is to bring togetherness to conquer the voices of silence.

To my Heavenly Father:

Thank you Father, for walking with me all the days of my life. Thank you for blessing me even when I may not have been a deserving servant. Thank you for blessing me when I deserved! Thank you for the path known and unknown. Thank you for the lessons taught and are being taught. Most importantly, thank you for the wisdom and strength to grow and become whole! AMEN

Made in the USA
Middletown, DE
25 April 2024

53482142R00080